SCOTT BROWNRIGG

SCOTT BROWNRIGG
ARCHITECTURE + PROGRESSION

Contents

7 Introduction

Darren Comber

18 Aviation

Aviation and globalization

Maurice Rosario and Chris Blow

44 Offices

Invigorating the workplace

Nick Ridout

68 Interior Design

Creating engaging internal environments

Beatriz Gonzalez

92 Business + Science Parks

The evolution of business parks to science parks

Ed Hayden

118 Rail

Creating infrastructure for seamless travel

Andrew Postings

140 Defence

Defence, the consideration of national security

Erika Gemmell

162 Education

Education for all: inspirational places to learn and grow

Ian Pratt and Helen Taylor

196 Residential + Mixed Use

Places to live and inhabit

Richard McCarthy

224 Future Thinking

Looking to the future

Darren Comber and Richard McCarthy

232 Contributors

233 Acknowledgements

234 Picture Credits

235 Index

Perspective
The philosophy of borrowed horizons

Architecture with inherent quality is produced not only through a well-defined process of rigorous design analysis, but also by harnessing the ability to convey that process and the ideas to the 'viewer'. Architecture should not be judged purely on the production of aesthetics. This alone is not a basis upon which to define architecture. It is not enough just to see architecture. You must experience it. It should be celebrated for its spatial qualities and for how it is attuned to the concept of achieving harmony in a specific area. A well-conceived masterplan or building will produce its own aesthetics that work with the language to sustain credibility and integrity. Architecture is produced partly as the product of its setting and through the circumstances requiring its conception.

Darren Comber

Introduction

Darren Comber
Chief Executive

The intent of this book is not simply to record the historical timeline of Scott Brownrigg, recounting the establishment of the practice and its later brand, but rather to investigate the evolution of an entity that has been robust and tenacious enough to keep moving forward with both purpose and direction over the last century. It is important to recognize that the cultural and business landscape has evolved in a series of events and movements that have witnessed a logarithmic advance in how the practice has designed and prescribed its own future.

Having an innate awareness of the big issues over the decades has permitted the Scott Brownrigg brand to metamorphose and grow into a hybrid business with architectural design at its core. Of course, not everything can be anticipated and planned for, but a mixture of good business acumen, intuition and sociocultural awareness has allowed for planned growth and for amelioration of *force majeure* and world events. The twenty-first century has seen the perceived shrinking of the globe owing to ease of travel and enhanced media connectivity; the growth of the bland and ubiquitous; and the loss of local identity. Increasing political instability has caused many things to change irreversibly. Enduring success is dependent on far more than the individual projects the practice has delivered.

Time is represented through change, and this is a constant. Thanks to its effective leadership and vision, and to its ability to adapt and be versatile and proactive rather than reactive, Scott Brownrigg has endured, evolved and progressed for over a century, and remains one of the leading architectural practices within the profession.

The early years

The humble beginnings of Scott Brownrigg can be traced back to 1910, when Annesley H. Brownrigg established a practice in the quaint market town of Haslemere in Surrey. Fast-forward to 2025 and the business is thriving, placed among the top twenty practices in the United Kingdom and among the top 100 architects on the world stage. Scott Brownrigg has evolved to look forward continually and to anticipate the challenges and opportunities that the future may bring. The birth of the practice predates the birth of modernism in Europe, which many historians recognize as the year 1922.

Annesley Brownrigg trained at the Architectural Association School of Architecture and in the offices of Ernest Newton, and in 1910 was the winner of a competition for Peterborough County School for Girls. He was an all-round architect with the ability to design all types of building. After serving in the Army during the First World War, Brownrigg returned to his practice in 1918 and initially earned a reputation for well-respected, traditional domestic work. The scope of his work expanded to include commercial and industrial buildings, local authority schools and better-quality housing schemes.

Annesley Brownrigg died in 1935, and Leslie Hiscock, with whom he had formed a partnership after the war, survived as the sole partner in the practice for two years. C.J. Morreau joined him in 1937, but unfortunately died at the end of the following year. At the beginning of 1939, Duncan Scott became a partner in the firm. Hiscock joined the RAF in August of the same year, on the brink of the Second World War, leaving Scott to run the practice. The war brought almost a complete stoppage of all school and private building work. The struggle to keep the practice going was eased only to a certain extent by Scott's teaching at the Architectural Association (AA). The bulk of the work resulted from bomb damage, and it was not until 1942 that the firm's workload improved with the introduction of projects from the Ministry of Works.

Meanwhile, Annesley's son John Brownrigg, who had only a loose association with his father's practice, had set up on his own after qualifying as an architect in 1936. The practice was developing on a modest scale when the war began, and the Royal Navy claimed his services. After John's demobilization at the end of the war, he met Newman Turner at a refresher course at the AA, and together they restarted the practice. Although Duncan Scott and John Brownrigg were old friends, they were competitors, and Scott ran his own practice independently from Brownrigg and Turner. It was not until 1955 that they decided to operate experimentally from London as a joint firm, while their respective studios in Guildford remained disassociated.

Finally, on 1 October 1958, the two practices amalgamated to form Scott Brownrigg & Turner, using this title in Guildford from 1958, in Woking from 1959, in London from 1961, in Glasgow from 1964, and in Peterborough from 1968.

The London experiment had shown that the very different personalities concerned got on well together, an important factor in any lifetime business association. The amalgamation was a success from the start, partly owing to the variety of approach and a diverse programme of work. Particularly significant was the fact that, separately, each firm had been capable of carrying out work of only a limited size, whereas this new combination brought new strength and the ability to work on major architectural programmes. Eventually this led to the practice designing the Queen Elizabeth Barracks, a significant project of its time that was opened in Guildford by Queen Elizabeth II on 30 October 1964.

The practice became one of the early pioneers of working internationally when it fulfilled the role of architect in a large consortium of structural engineers, quantity surveyors and others set up in Pakistan under the title of Associated British Consultants. Established in 1961, the consortium provided a fully comprehensive service.

As the practice expanded, a problem emerged: the architects neglected the vital task of managing themselves. Fortunately, one of the partners had a high degree of administrative ability and devoted his entire time to managing the practice – a model that has been part of the enduring success of the firm across the decades.

In 1968 the partners of Scott Brownrigg & Turner wrote:

In planning for the future, there are two important factors. The first is the continuity of the firm by planning well in advance for the retirement of partners from full active control (though not from participation), and the second, that the firm should not lose its personal identity, least of all a firm giving such a personal service as architecture.

Finally, there is one thing, and one thing alone, that is very much part of the service to a client which is of paramount importance, [that] extends even beyond that service because it affects many people in addition to the building owner, and indeed future generations as well, and that is the creation of good architecture and a satisfying environment.

The transition to SBT

The practice was originally established as a partnership, and this changed only in 1993, when it was incorporated into a limited company operating with an employee benefit trust. The transition to a limited company was born out of circumstance – a recession that affected many practices – rather than out of a desire for structural change or transfer of ownership. In the 1980s Scott Brownrigg & Turner had enjoyed significant growth, which led to it becoming the second-largest architecture practice in the UK. However, such growth was unsustainable in the long term, and with the recession of the early 1990s and the retirement of some senior partners, the practice endured financial stress, to the extent that restructuring was necessary to ensure survival.

The change of structure also led to a name change for the practice, and for many years to follow the firm used the abbreviation SBT.

Becoming Scott Brownrigg

As the practice developed its international footprint of projects, so grew the desire and requirement to develop and maintain a clearly identifiable brand. Since the 1960s, the brand name Scott Brownrigg & Turner had been well known across the globe on account of the company's work abroad at a time when most architects rarely left their own shores. However, SBT as a brand was relatively unknown outside the UK, and the use of the dual names became increasingly confusing to clients. Branding consultants were engaged at the beginning of the twenty-first century, and the decision was made to use only one brand name – a shortened version of the practice's full name. In both the international and domestic markets, the business would be known as Scott Brownrigg.

Following the first foray overseas, in Pakistan in the early 1960s, the practice went on to work on projects around the world, from New Zealand to Los Angeles. In the 1970s Scott Brownrigg was

Historic signage shows how the practice and its brand evolved from 1939 to the 1990s.

among the first of many foreign practices to work in the Middle East, designing everything from airports in Iraq to new islands in Abu Dhabi.

The fact it had an international platform allowed the practice to be resilient to the vagaries of the UK market. During this time, Scott Brownrigg was working on a number of leisure developments throughout the Mediterranean, and so undertook a recruitment drive to ensure that it had staff fluent in most European languages. For a number of years, the practice had a studio in Harare, Zimbabwe, and worked across Africa. Ownership of the studio in Cyprus was transferred in 2008, but the practice remains active on the island.

The alchemy of growth

In Covent Garden there is a beautiful merchant's shop. As you gaze at the finery in the window, you are drawn in. It is open and welcoming to everybody, but it is a special club, and when you get inside you find that, although you may not desire what you originally saw in the window, just by simply being in there you discover many other things that you might like to acquire and experience. It is all about expanding horizons through interaction and experience – a philosophy that underpins much of Scott Brownrigg's work and approach to remaining relevant as a practice.

Scott Brownrigg's history traces an undulating line marked by dynamic changes of fortune: sequential steps, forward motion, and momentum that has significantly increased since the end of the last century. The secret of success is to be proactive rather than reactive. Analytical and intuitive methods have allowed the practice to move forward via calculated anticipation based on an understanding of the cultural backdrop and its measurable definitions as described in architectural commissions.

Running parallel to the timeline of Scott Brownrigg have been fluctuations in the economic cycle and sociopolitical changes. Equally significant for the practice have been enormous strides in technical innovation.

During the late 1980s, Scott Brownrigg & Turner recognized the need to provide specialist services, including such specialist divisions as SBT Project Management and SBT Planning. SBT Project Management was a short-lived service, but the specialist town-planning service continued for two decades, and ceased as an embedded service only when the competition from external town-planning companies no longer made it viable.

Scott Brownrigg has always recognized the need to embrace change and to see it as an opportunity. The acquisition in 2004 of Design Research Unit (DRU) – which brought with it prestige and original thinking – is an example of how the brand has evolved and become stronger. The DRU acquisition has proved catalytic for the development of the business model that now drives Scott Brownrigg. The theme of the 'unit' has been one of the most important directions implemented by the leaders of the practice over the past three decades, ensuring both vertical and horizontal expansion of service offerings.

Added businesses and services have met the requirement for change and helped Scott Brownrigg to secure longevity and relevancy, whether it be through acknowledging the demand for digital twins by establishing Digital Twin Unit; providing the technical expertise to deliver buildings designed either by the practice or by other practices through Design Delivery Unit; assisting in the effective management of the early design process through Design Management Unit; understanding the requirements of buildings and assessing how they will be used through Design Strategy Unit; or addressing health and safety across the industry through Safety Design Unit.

This approach represents a direct and 'smart' offering to a widening client base in the context of the speed, agility and precision that are needed today. Historically, the ideal architect was seen as a 'universal' person with expertise spread across innumerable disciplines. To an extent, this view has now changed, and a deeper understanding of niche speciality is required. The multiple threads of expertise necessary to design and deliver projects are more complex than ever and demand simplification through having the right people in the right place on the right project at the right time.

Enduring success depends on much more than individual projects. It comes from challenging the business model from within and asking questions. Curiosity is a key driver and component. There is an inherent belief in the business that heritage gives the practice both credibility and authenticity. But this is not to say that Scott Brownrigg is bound to history; indeed, there is no place for sentimentality in the company's brand.

Such prominent twentieth-century brands as Mini and Burberry have modernized their image by taking on and absorbing cultural and technical values, and over the decades Scott Brownrigg has sought to do the same. Established businesses have built-in legacy systems that are harder to transform, and newer organizations can leapfrog older players. The practice has always asked the question: how can we serve clients on their terms in a fast-moving, interconnected industry?

Heritage can be an advantage only if it does not provide the basis for continual extraction. The key metrics are based on shared purpose, innovation, communication and experience. Underperformance in any of these variables can lead to frailty, and the ability to adopt and adapt has been central to the more recent history of the practice. Dyson's innovation is rooted in solving the everyday frustrations in people's lives. A respect for research and innovation has led to a culture of boldness, measured risk-taking to learn from potential outcomes, and perfect problem-solving strategies. Collaboration lies at the heart of Scott Brownrigg's longevity, as does an enthusiasm for innovation that is always client-focused. The future is based on a clear vision, agility, talent, succession-planning and investment in technology and people.

Brand perception in architecture can run deep and be tribal. Perception can become reality when people have not engaged with the practice, and considerable work has been undertaken to shift perceptions where any realignment of the past is required. It is vital not to appear parochial, and the best way to expand is to authentically use the inherent DNA. One example is the adoption and interpretation of timber-framed prefabricated housing projects, which became an integral part of the business in the 1960s and a precursor to much of what has been seen more recently in the profession. Many of the practice's current projects employ unitized panelling and modular systems throughout their design and realization, enhancing and streamlining on-site processing and ensuring quality control in the finished building.

Iconic architecture becomes part of a cultural landscape, whereas ordinary buildings offer few historical reference points for commentators to uphold. A pivotal project in Scott Brownrigg's early history is the Yvonne Arnaud Theatre in Guildford, completed in 1965 and now Grade II listed. This building provides irrefutable evidence that both style and substance are at the heart of the design process and product. Scott Brownrigg's projects have followed in this tradition, whether in aviation, advanced technology, commercial offices, residential or the many other sectors in which the practice works.

The practice has consistently focused on how process and product are inextricably linked. The competition-winning design for Terminal 4 at Heathrow Airport (pp. 26–27) in 1977 involved the introduction of computer-aided design (CAD) as part of the production-information sequence. This was a groundbreaking development, and at the time Scott Brownrigg was leading the way as one of the first practices to embrace CAD, using

Yvonne Arnaud Theatre
Aerial photograph of the Grade II-listed Yvonne Arnaud Theatre in Guildford, originally designed by John Brownrigg and completed in 1965.

the software GDS (later known as MicroGDS) to design buildings. The practice continued to use MicroGDS, which in later years rivalled the mainstream software programs AutoCAD and MicroStation.

Terminal 2 at Manchester Airport was quick to follow the opening of Heathrow Terminal 4, as was the commission for the BBC at White City. This important trio of projects gave the practice momentum, resilience and expertise, prepared the way for a widening of typologies, and provided a deeper understanding of the socioeconomic complexities of larger, more significant commissions.

Adherence to the central tenet of process informing product and to the goal of clear and legible simplicity informed the work completed from the 1960s through to the 1990s. Scott Brownrigg avoided the style wars that developed in the latter part of this period by following formalistic and pragmatic attitudes to design. Modernism shifted to postmodernism, and these decades witnessed the growth of classical pastiche, abstracted motifs, split pediments and the addition of Chippendale tops to skyscrapers. While many architects believed that florid architraves, enormous keystones and pastel shades would be more palatable for urban intervention in the UK, it was a stylistic direction that Scott Brownrigg had no interest in following.

To a certain extent, the British predilection for nostalgia and the picturesque was responsible for setting the practice apart from the white heat of the European schools during the birth of modernism in the 1920s. Decades later, Scott Brownrigg was wary of the expressions of postmodernism, and once again this attitude can be attributed to a focus on the inextricable link between process and product. Similarly, Scott Brownrigg did not follow the British school of gothic high tech, which saw English architects exporting highly engineered and overtly complex structures that, although contemporary, looked back at the great Victorian age of Paxton and Brunel.

There is not only one worthy approach, at the exclusion of all others, to achieving an architectural edifice. Architecture is an art form, and exceptional design is often produced by ephemeral influences that inform and affect people's everyday lives, which change over time. The key is to develop a process of analysis, to unlock these influences and to design from a conceptual framework that is credible and referential, and can justifiably be supported to bring value.

The practice defined its own space not by seeking to follow current trends, nor by establishing a referential design 'signature' across its projects, but by seeking to deliver within a framework of its own principles. Emphasis has been placed on rigorous analysis, quality of thought and the quality of the details. How a building looks can be subjective, but the practice has always striven to be known for quality of product and design, and for buildings or places that have longevity rather than short-term fashion appeal.

Architectural sobriety enabled the Scott Brownrigg team to make the transition through to the year 2000, when it developed and occupied its own premises in Guildford. Work was won on process-driven analysis and the ability to deliver this in-built form. The interest in 'making' and, by default, in craft was there at the very start of the Scott Brownrigg journey, and it can be seen as a common thread through the decades. The acquisition of Design Research Unit (DRU) was an astute move, reinforcing the belief in form and function, and offering elegant solutions to the design puzzles that Scott Brownrigg faced. An outstanding and radical agency that changed the direction of industrial design, particularly in the 1960s, DRU was an entirely natural fit for the practice.

DRU was the first consultancy to combine architecture, graphics and industrial design, and has shaped the nature of the built environment for more than eighty years. In many ways the British Bauhaus, this agency understood the central components of and thinking behind modernism. Scott Brownrigg is now able to draw directly on the extraordinary legacy of the original DRU, and has leveraged its practical and philosophical thinking to guide ongoing project work. This is an agile and interactive part of the current business, one that enables open discussion and critique across the practice. The resonance of this unit has a positive, energizing influence on multiple projects developed in the practice's international studios, whether in New York, Singapore or Amsterdam.

Scott Brownrigg recognized a further opportunity to add skills and broaden its sector experience in 2015, when it was approached by Gollins Melvin Ward (GMW; founded 1947) to acquire the practice. There was a chronological synergy with the work of GMW, particularly in the 1960s. Notable projects by the practice in the 1950s included Castrol House in Marylebone, one of the first uses of curtain walling on a frame construction in the UK, and the central campus at the University of Sheffield, especially the Arts Tower.

GMW was an ardent follower of the modernist architectural movement that was developed by Walter Gropius and Ludwig Mies van der Rohe at the Bauhaus in Germany and subsequently in the United States. GMW's twenty-eight-storey Commercial Union Tower, completed in 1969, was groundbreaking: the first building in the City of London to exceed the height of St Paul's Cathedral. For the purist, this was the height of well-proportioned restraint, and the tower stood for more than fifty years between emerging skyscrapers over twice its height. It was radical not only for its aesthetics, but also for its innovative structure and construction method. Rather than being supported from ground level,

Commercial Union Tower
After its completion in 1969, the Commercial Union Tower won a Civic Trust Award and the 1970 Structural Steel Design Award.

the individual floors were hung via steel rods from cantilevers extending out from the central core.

Another important GMW project of relevance to Scott Brownrigg was the BOAC Terminal at JFK Airport in New York – a precursor of the current business's significant presence in the international aviation sector. Commissioned in 1963, the terminal was based on minimal and direct travel routes for passengers, ease and flexibility of logistics and management, and reliable and efficient baggage-handling services. The simple brutalist building with dynamic sloping facades was elegant and functional, and used radical solutions to boarding bridges for the iconic Boeing 747. After the merger of BOAC and BEA in 1974 to create British Airways, the terminal hosted the start of supersonic services at JFK with a dedicated lounge for Concorde passengers.

The design principles embodied by such projects aligned entirely with the values of Scott Brownrigg, and in 2015 the decision was taken to fully integrate GMW into the practice and for it to operate under the Scott Brownrigg brand.

The acquisition of other practices required additional studio space to accommodate the growth of Scott Brownrigg. While Scott Brownrigg's established home was in Guildford, the practice had had a number of studio locations in the capital since first setting up a London office in 1961, all of them in Covent Garden; this area has now been the second home of the practice for some sixty-five years. Initially renting space and moving locations to suit demand, Scott Brownrigg eventually acquired 77 Endell Street in 2006 and remains there two decades later.

It should be acknowledged that, in the early years, the sectors and building 'typologies' for which Scott Brownrigg was most renowned were more limited, and the bandwidth has varied dramatically over the decades. In the 1980s the practice was known predominantly for business parks and airports, but expertise has expanded widely to embrace all sectors: offices, residential and mixed use, aviation and rail, defence and security, education and health, digital, culture, media and sport, alongside involvement in major masterplanning programmes that have the ability to provide significant societal change.

Over the decades, there has been a shift in attitude towards caring for the environment. Scott Brownrigg was interested in this facet of design before it became a fundamental requirement of the design process. Concern for the environment was an early USP of the practice, which in 2000 was appointed to design the new headquarters for the Environment Agency at Wallingford, Oxfordshire (pp. 52–55). The building led the way in terms of deployable environmental design and, at the time of its completion in 2005, became the focus of attention at a British Council for Offices conference in Paris, where Scott Brownrigg spoke about the merits of passive environmental design. The practice was then commissioned to design the headquarters for the Centre for Agriculture and Bioscience International (CABI; pp. 64–65), a project that expanded on the established principles to deliver a building at one with its surroundings.

Since this time, the practice has continually striven to further both research into and demonstrable deployment of sustainable techniques for construction and occupation of buildings. Part of this initiative has involved establishing the annual RIBA Scott Brownrigg Award for Sustainable Development, which was launched in 2022 to explore and research the broad spectrum of what is meant by sustainable design within communities.

Another key area of interest for the practice over the years has been the role of the architect as masterplanner and urban designer. In the late 1980s Scott Brownrigg designed two striking glass-and-steel sail-shaped towers, forty-six and thirty-six storeys high respectively. Dubbed 'Twin Peaks' by the media and totalling over 185,000 square metres, the towers were intended to act as a catalyst for the extension of London's Central Business District (CBD) at Heron Quays in the Docklands. At the same time, César Pelli was designing a tower for Olympia & York with the same purpose, but on a different Docklands site. The government of Margaret Thatcher favoured the alternative site, and One Canada Square became the first building to complete at the newly established CBD Canary Wharf. An interesting thought, had the Scott Brownrigg proposal gone ahead: it could have completely changed the face of London.

Having designed offices for over a century, Scott Brownrigg has inevitably experienced pivotal moments in the history and development not only of the workplace, but also of the towns and cities around it. Perhaps one of the most notable interventions was when the practice was commissioned to design a small building in the City of London in 1997. The project created an opportunity to explore the role of urban design

BOAC Terminal, JFK Airport
The flat, overhanging concrete roof of JFK's BOAC Terminal was originally designed to accommodate passenger helicopter services to Manhattan.

Dining Wall Café
The Dining Wall Café concept of 1997 offered an opportunity to enhance a key historic and commercial location in the City of London.

and how people interact with one another – that is, to study human behaviour. Although the Dining Wall Café on Cheapside was compact in size, qualities encouraging social interaction embodied in its design went on to form the basis of design exploration in significant masterplans across the world.

The main challenges in terms of growth over the years have required a measured plan for steady expansion, rather than rapid growth and then inevitable downsizing when markets change because of economic cycles. This approach has served the practice well and allowed Scott Brownrigg to retain talent as a result. Adding skills and sectors through acquisition has also been a vital part of this plan.

The key desire for the future of Scott Brownrigg is to see the practice remain relevant and continue to make a contribution to society. Scott Brownrigg has always aimed to be a practice where individuals can flourish and express themselves as architects and designers; where they can develop their careers in a way that enables them to create something special and make a positive contribution to the built environment.

The most important goal for the practice is to continue to serve clients and to design meaningful projects that have a legacy to effect positive change on the built environment.

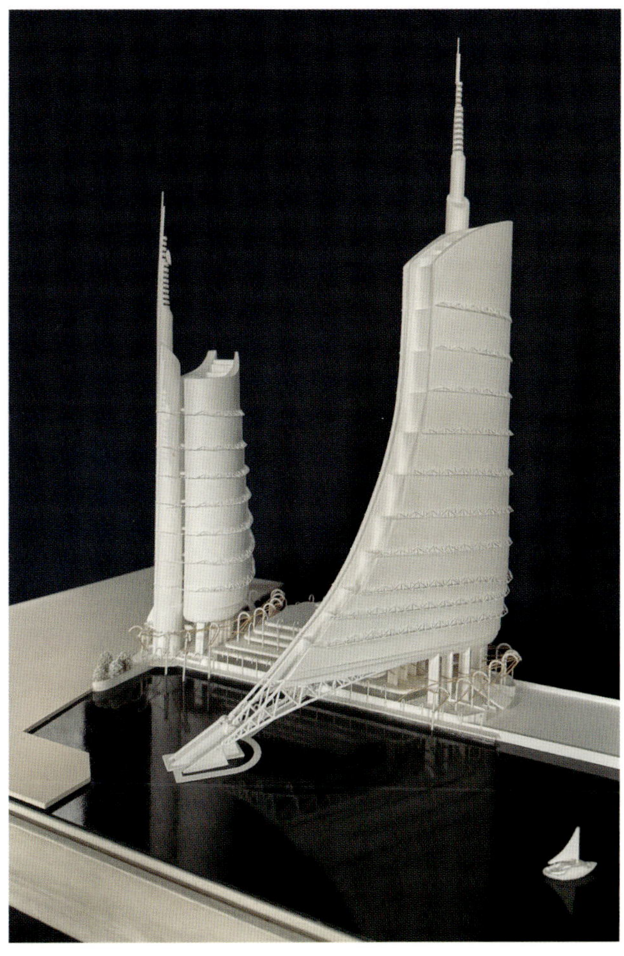

Heron Quays Towers
A model of the Heron Quays Towers, their mast and sail structures reflective of the site's context and history.

Aviation

Aviation and globalization

Maurice Rosario
and Chris Blow

Airport design has had a significant role to play in the growth and development of Scott Brownrigg, particularly in the early 1980s, when the practice secured work on some of the largest airports in the UK. During this period, the then Scott Brownrigg & Turner grew to more than 400 employees, becoming one of the UK's largest architectural practices. The airport commissions firmly placed the practice on the map as a leading aviation architect and paved the way for future high-profile projects around the world.

The practice's involvement in airports began in 1976, with the commission by the British Airports Authority (BAA) to act as 'house architects' for replanning the international area and catering facilities at Heathrow Terminal 1. Shortly afterwards came the invitation to take part in the Terminal 4 limited competition (pp. 26–27). As a result of continued growth in the air-travel industry, Heathrow Airport, the world's busiest international airport, needed to increase its capacity to 38 million passengers a year through the addition of a fourth terminal. Some 2000 passengers per hour would pass through its doors. Vertical segregation of arrivals and departures, combined with negating the need for gate assembly enclosures, was a major innovation in airport design, representing a move away from the traditional departure lounge.

For the previous thirty years, Heathrow Airport had been the hub of world civil aviation; it was felt that a fully integrated four-terminal system would guarantee that it held this position in the future. With this desire, planning for the new terminal began in 1973. Four years later, the BAA submitted a planning application to the Greater London Council for a site on the airport's south side, and the go-ahead was given in December 1979.

As Mike King, director of Heathrow Airport, stated at the time: 'The British Airports Authority are not only the owners and operators of the airport, but as world leaders in airport planning and design we are providing a terminal for the future with the hallmarks of Space, Speed, Simplicity and Service.'

These hallmarks mirrored the design parameters proposed in Scott Brownrigg's winning concept, which was selected over those of four bigger London-based firms. The practice worked with the engineers SWK and DSSR, and Heathrow Terminal 4 was built under an innovative management contract. The work necessary to bring the design from a simple concept to full delivery involved 35,000 major design and engineering drawings, with extensive investment in and use of state-of-the-art computer-aided-design (CAD) techniques and systems by the practice.

A four-year construction programme proved an enormous challenge. The BAA appointed a management contractor to manage and coordinate construction. This involved 700 individual contracts, ranging in value from a few hundred pounds to many millions, and incorporated 49,000 square metres of external cladding and 13,000 tonnes of structural steel works. As site activity reached its peak in 1983, expenditure levels escalated to over £1 million a week (£4.5 million today), and the workforce increased from 650 to 1100 to ensure the terminal would be operational in 1985 and brought within the budget of £200 million.

Meanwhile, in 1982, construction of the Terminal 4 Piccadilly line Underground station began, enabling airport passengers to travel beneath the airport, first to the new Terminal 4, then to Terminals 1, 2 and 3. As quoted in the *Daily Telegraph* on 11 March 1986, the scheme comprised '£22m investment, a departure concourse one-third of a mile long, the biggest baggage carousels in the world and up to 60 people working on the plans at one time, half of them architects'.

Terminal 4 was officially opened on 1 April 1986 by the Prince and Princess of Wales. At the opening ceremony, Prince Charles noted it as a 'substantially British achievement, and as such it represents a national success story'. Some 800 guests joined the royal couple at lunch in the departure lounge, with a Boeing 747 and Concorde parked close by. The terminal was ranked the best UK airport by readers of *Condé Nast Traveller* magazine, also coming out top in Europe and fourth favourite in the world. On 25 May 1984, *The Times* commented, 'The new terminal advances thinking on airport planning around the world.'

The late entry of British Airways as the occupant of Terminal 4, in place of American Airlines, led to relations with its project team and to Scott Brownrigg's subsequent appointment to

Terminal 4, Heathrow Airport
At the time of construction, Heathrow Terminal 4 was one of the largest single building contracts undertaken in the UK.

the Birmingham 'Eurohub' scheme in 1988, and to the Air Russia hub at Moscow Domodedovo in 1990. The innovative designs predominantly supported 'in-transit' passengers looking to take advantage of multiple routes across the UK and Europe, in the case of Birmingham; and across the world on the great circle linking the eastern United States and Europe with the Far East, in the case of Moscow. Birmingham was built by a design-and-build contractor, while the Moscow Domodedovo hub was cancelled owing to the collapse of the Soviet Union.

Following the opening of Terminal 4, Scott Brownrigg worked on the Manchester Airport Terminal 2 competition, which was won in January 1989 and completed in 1993, on time and on budget. After planning approval, a project office was set up on-site with CAD, so that all design work could be carried out with the client team close by.

Manchester Airport's first terminal, together with the domestic pier, opened in May 1989, and had a capacity of 12 million passengers per year. The first phase of the new Terminal 2 opened in 1993 and was Manchester's answer to providing additional long-haul routes, many of which might otherwise have been routed via one of the overcrowded airports in southeast England. Site constraints determined that the first phase comprised mostly a central terminal and a long single-sided pier. From the elevated departures forecourt to check-in, outbound controls and then the airside concourse, passengers have a level route.

While working on Terminal 4 at Heathrow, Scott Brownrigg was appointed with the British engineers Maunsell to work on Baghdad and Basra airports in Iraq. In 1978, following a fallout with the original winners of the project, the Iraqi State Organization for Roads and Bridges asked the UK government for urgent help, and the government recommended the practice. The Iraqi state needed the airports to complete in time for the Non-Aligned Movement conference in Baghdad in 1982 (the conference was subsequently relocated to Delhi for fear of bombing in Baghdad). With three modular terminals, Baghdad International Airport, previously known as Saddam International Airport, became the largest international airport in Iraq and marked the start of decades of aviation work for the practice in the Middle East.

While working on the two main Iraqi projects, Scott Brownrigg was also commissioned to design a new terminal (unbuilt) for Erbil Airport in Kurdistan, part of an Iraqi government initiative to aid the Kurdish community at the time of the Iran–Iraq War. With a dusk-to-dawn wartime curfew, the site visit was challenging and resulted in an overnight stay on the heavily trafficked Silk Road crossing northern Iraq.

Work on the Bahrain Airport extension followed in 1985 with Scott Wilson Kirkpatrick. A combination of complicated phasing and working with a local contractor slowed the project: the extension opened in 1991, and the original airport was refurbished in 1993. As in the case of Heathrow Terminal 4, the design incorporated segregated departure and arrivals, and was soon heralded as 'the best facility in the Gulf'.

The practice continued to seek out overseas airport opportunities during the 1990s, particularly in Southeast Asia. The award of second place in a competition to design Hong Kong's new international airport at Chek Lap Kok in 1991 led to the opening of a local project office in 1992 and the design of a number of projects for Hong Kong-based airline Cathay Pacific – a notable example of aviation development driven by a political situation, before the British handover of Hong Kong to China in 1997. Another project aimed to encourage post-war tourism on the coast of Vietnam at Nha Trang using the former US air base at Cam Ranh. The practice would revisit Vietnam in 2016 to enter a competition to masterplan Long Thanh Airport.

In France, Scott Brownrigg teamed up with the local architects Curtelin Ricard Bergeret and Bureau d'Études Technip to effectively rebuild

Terminal 2 at Lyon-Saint Exupéry Airport for the Chamber of Commerce. Works commenced in 1991 and completed in 2002 after multiphase construction, increasing airport capacity from 4 million to 8 million passengers per year.

Work in Saudi Arabia started in 2012 with Prince Mohammad bin Abdulaziz International Airport (Medina Airport), with a brief to prepare a new masterplan (pp. 30–33). Completed in 2015, Terminal 1 was the first commercial airport terminal to become LEED Gold certified in the Middle East and North Africa region. The project was designed to be delivered over three phases and to eventually accommodate up to 17 million passengers per year. The subsequent phase started in 2024, creating a new Terminal 2 and renovating the existing Terminal 3 to cater for Hajj and Umrah charter flights.

In 2018 the practice carried out the major renovation of King Khalid International Airport in Riyadh, Saudi Arabia. The project also included the creation of Terminal 5, designed initially to cater for domestic traffic and then be switched to international operations when domestic traffic is relocated to Terminal 1. The terminal roof is a modern reflection of the iconic design of the existing terminals 1, 2, 3 and 4.

The practice has since been appointed to work on new terminal buildings at Al-Qassim, Hail and Taif airports in Saudi Arabia. Each is designed to reflect the region's culture and heritage, while promoting a unique sense of place and destination.

Terminal 3, Cairo Airport
Working within the original envelope design for Terminal 3 at Cairo Airport led to a number of innovative solutions for the new-build design.

Istanbul Airport
Within the first year of operation, Istanbul Airport achieved LEED Gold certification and was officially registered as the largest LEED-certified terminal building worldwide.

The acquisition of GMW in 2015 presented an opportunity to grow Scott Brownrigg's aviation team and to bring together decades of international aviation experience under one roof. GMW's portfolio included the 1960s design for the BOAC (now BA) Terminal at JFK Airport, New York; Istanbul Atatürk Airport; Terminal 3 at Cairo Airport, which provides a hub for EgyptAir's international and domestic flights; Terminal 2 at Antalya Airport, Turkey; and, at the point of joining Scott Brownrigg, the new Istanbul Airport, planned to be the largest airport in the world.

Designed in 2005 as part of the BAA Framework, a 200-metre-long pedestrian bridge at Gatwick Airport connects the North Terminal to a new Pier 6 (pp. 28–29). High enough to allow a Boeing 747 to pass beneath, the bridge spans a live aircraft taxiway and was therefore assembled off-site and moved into position in just three days using specialist heavy-lifting techniques. The bridge was named Major Project of the Year in the 2006 Quality in Construction Awards and has since become a landmark feature at the airport.

Anticipating the introduction of the Airbus A380, the renovation of Heathrow Terminal 3 in 2006 included the delivery of a new Pier 6 with wider stands, taxiways and runways to accommodate the large new-generation aircraft. With an inherent understanding of operational strategies and passenger flow, the team created a new set of design guidelines to ensure safe and quick embarkation and disembarkation of a large number of passengers. These guidelines have since been rolled out on the refurbishment and design of new airports across the world.

Throughout its history of working on airports, Scott Brownrigg has sought to sensitively embed these schemes into the cultural setting by incorporating local design features and styles. Roofs with large overhangs were created for the Bangkok competition in 1993 and Kuala Lumpur Sepang in 1992; and historic forms, including reinterpretations of fifteenth-century Great Zimbabwe ruins, for the Harare competition in 1995. The design for Diori Hamani International Airport in Niger (completed 2019) was inspired by Nigerien circular mud houses, and within the terminal incorporates a permanent museum display showcasing three of the oldest dinosaur fossils found in the region.

The design for Istanbul Airport (pp. 34–37), which opened in 2019, was inspired by its vibrant city, with a modern take on classic Turkish architecture and the ever-changing hues and tones of Istanbul reflected in the interior design. While the airport is considered an architectural feat, its swift build was achieved through a fast decision-making process made possible by all design, construction and client teams working collaboratively under one roof. This approach, coupled with off-site manufacturing, enabled the delivery of two runways, a 90-million-passenger terminal, and ancillary buildings in just three years.

In 2019 the aviation team's design focus returned to Heathrow, working on a commission by the Arora Group to create an alternative scheme for the Heathrow expansion: the Terminal 6 campus known as Heathrow West (pp. 38–41). The return to Heathrow has allowed Scott Brownrigg's current and future thinking to be embedded into the design, with sustainable innovations that benefit not only passengers but also the wider community.

Heathrow West, Heathrow Airport
Designs for the proposed new Terminal 6 at Heathrow Airport incorporate a multimodal interchange, allowing passengers to arrive by train, bus, car or bicycle.

Terminal 4, Heathrow Airport

Hillingdon, London
Completed 1986

The practice won the bid to design the £200 million Heathrow Terminal 4 in 1977. It led to advancements in airport thinking across the globe.

At the time of completion in 1986, prior to the Channel Tunnel, Heathrow Terminal 4 – costing £200 million – was the biggest building project in the UK.

The terminal building itself was 97,000 square metres. Despite severe height restrictions, it was designed to offer complete vertical segregation, with arrivals and departures located on separate floor levels. This separation – together with a 650-metre-long, 25-metre-wide airside departures concourse, housing all passenger facilities and without gate assembly enclosures – allowed for an increased speed of passenger flows, and for trolleys to be taken right to the boarding point. Such major innovation provided a number of benefits and represented a move away from the traditional departure lounge, which comprised lengthy, dull corridors and sterile, enclosed gate rooms.

The concourse design – at the time, the longest in the world – encouraged passengers to spend more time airside, taking advantage of duty-free and tax-paid shopping in a relaxed, tree-lined boulevard with cafes, bars and shops, visible boarding points and reassuring views of aircraft. It also achieved a major aim of the scheme – namely, that passengers could travel through the building either on the level or in a downward direction. These movements were facilitated by generous ramps, lifts, escalators and 500 metres of moving walkways.

There was a desired objective to park the maximum number of wide-bodied aircraft directly at the terminal. On its opening, Terminal 4 had 80 per cent of its stands served, in contrast to just 60 per cent at other terminals. The apron layout was future-proofed to allow for the advent of aircraft with a maximum wingspan of 70 metres, length of 86 metres and tail height of 21 metres.

The landside departures concourse was designed to accommodate eighty-four check-in desks in a single line, to ensure identification of appropriate check-in points, with generous queuing and circulation areas. Landside commercial facilities were deliberately kept to a minimum to encourage passengers to move airside and alleviate congestion.

The new terminal – considered the flagship terminal for the airport – was planned to serve international long-haul flights, to relieve pressure on Terminal 3. British Airways operated the supersonic aircraft Concorde out of the terminal.

Pier 6, London Gatwick Airport

Crawley, West Sussex
Completed 2005

Pier 6 at London Gatwick Airport was designed to facilitate an increase in processing capacity at the North Terminal. A new satellite pier would be linked to the terminal via a prefabricated passenger bridge that spanned a live taxiway.

The brief presented several challenges: the pier bridge would have to be sufficiently wide and high to allow a Boeing 747-400 aircraft to pass safely underneath, and its construction would have to take place with limited taxiway closure. Modular design technology was therefore adopted to reduce work on-site and ensure speed of construction. The 200-metre clear-span bridge was built off-site and craned in over a few nights, with minimal disruption to airport services.

There were no aircraft stands beyond the bridge that could accommodate Airbus A380s, so the bridge did not need to be as high as it was built. However, the scheme was the first outside the United States to span an airport taxiway, and the first in the UK to apply this scale of prefabrication in an airport setting. Creating a major landmark for Gatwick, the bridge facilitates a unique experience and perspective of the airport for the millions of passengers who pass above the operational taxiway.

To minimize impact on the airport operation, the bridge was built off-site in three sections and craned into place in as many days.

Prince Mohammad bin Abdulaziz International Airport

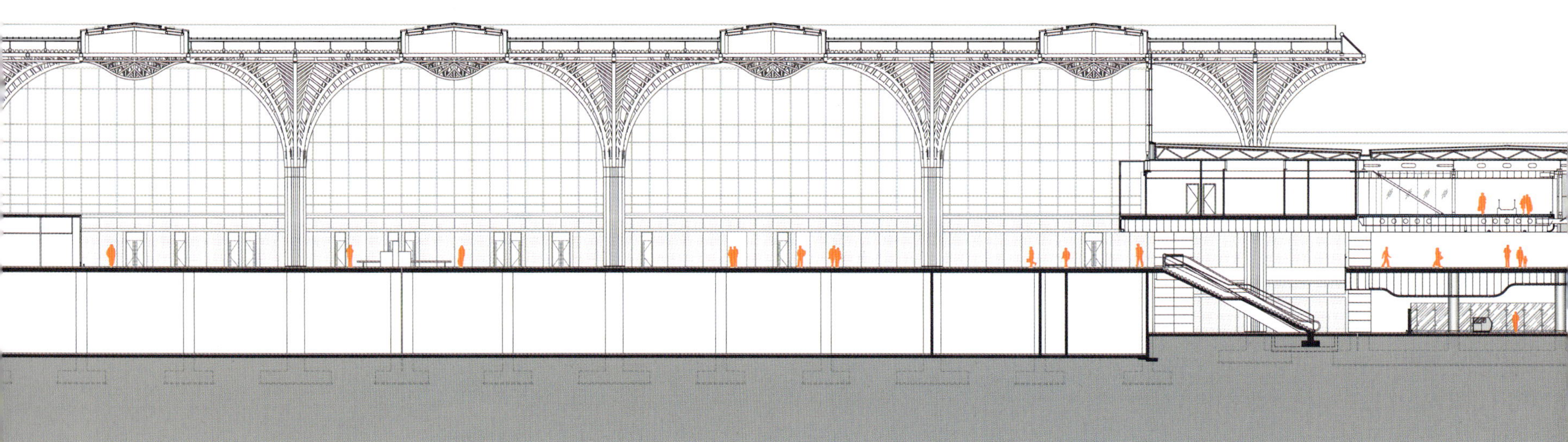

Medina, Saudi Arabia
Completed 2015

Designed by Scott Brownrigg in 2012, the masterplan for the airport's expansion involved relocation of the airport campus to the eastern side of an existing runway system, to allow for future runways on both sides of a new midfield terminal campus. Proposals included a new 150,000-square-metre terminal building, Hajj pavilions, a mosque, hotel, flight-catering building, logistic centre and central utility campus. New landside and airside infrastructure includes a new road network, taxiway and aprons, as well as ancillary buildings, runway rehabilitation, and aircraft rescue and fire-fighting facilities.

The design concept was inspired by the airport's role as a gateway for millions of Islamic pilgrims and by the palm tree, a symbol of peace and welcome employed as a motif throughout the terminal building. The palm brings a unique architectural identity to the development, and an interpretation of the palm frond provides a pragmatic and efficient structural support while using a minimal amount of material. Medina Airport was the first commercial airport terminal to become LEED Gold certified in the Middle East and North Africa region.

Twelve years later, the practice was appointed to design a second terminal and associated facilities in order to double the capacity of the airport, increasing current throughput to 17 million passengers per annum.

The overarching design philosophy integrates the key principles of Islamic art and architecture, emphasizing geometric patterns, light and space. Aerial view: Google Earth, 2025 Airbus. Below: Section through the terminal and gates.

Prince Mohammad bin Abdulaziz International Airport
The distinctive modular steel palm-tree columns of the original design have been developed to provide a more modern and efficient solution for the expansion scheme.

Istanbul Airport

Istanbul, Turkey
Completed 2019

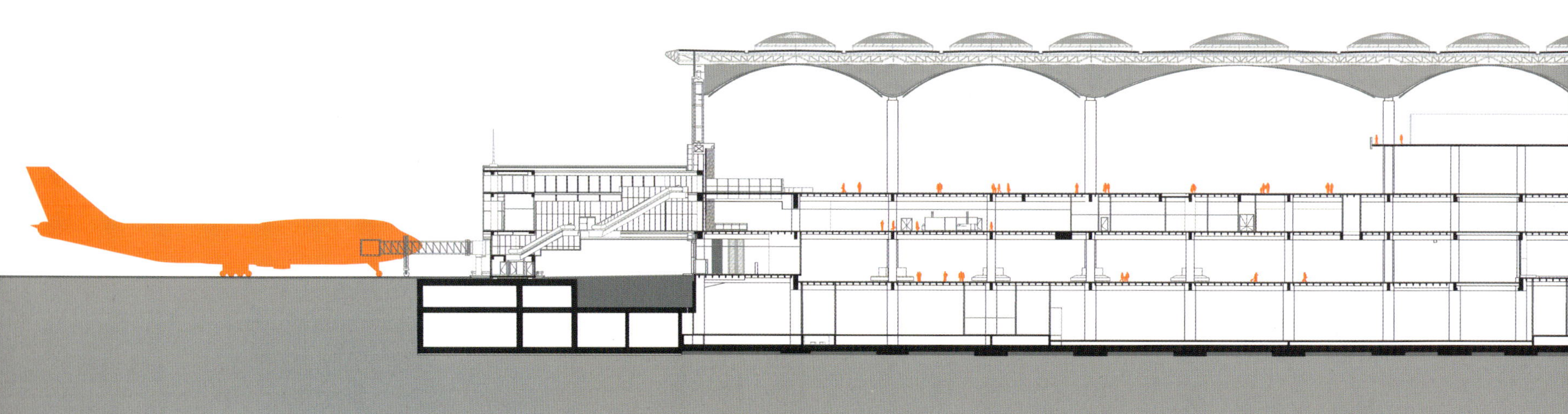

Istanbul Airport has the largest single terminal under one roof in the world. The airport completed in 2019, creating an iconic transport hub for Istanbul while improving connectivity between Turkey and the rest of the world.

The terminal is organized over two and a half levels, creating an efficient and flexible processor that can be expanded easily, both within its current envelope and, if required, by extending either side.

Acting as a grand gateway to Turkey, the scheme captures the cultural influences of Istanbul; simple but rich forms combine to create an elegant building inspired by the work of the Ottoman architect Mimar Sinan. The terminal integrates grand spaces and smaller areas to produce variety in scale along the passenger journey, with vaulted ceilings reinforcing a sense of direction from landside to airside. Ring-shaped skylights bring diffused natural daylight through the ceiling, creating lofty and atmospheric spaces. The light patterns they cast during the day are echoed by LED halos that produce the same effect at night.

The airport provides an iconic transport hub with a gross area of 1.4 million square metres and an initial capacity of 90 million passengers per year.

Istanbul Airport won the Future Projects – Infrastructure Award at the World Architecture Festival in 2016. Below: Section through the terminal and gates.

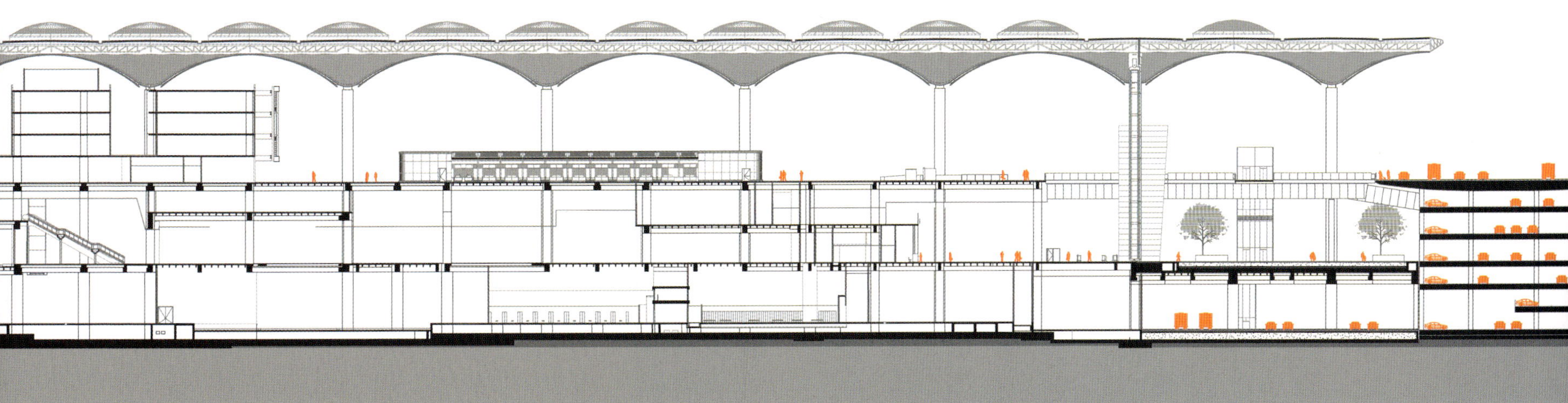

Istanbul Airport
Points of interest and landmarks aid wayfinding and enhance the passenger experience. The vaulted ceiling is inspired by Turkey's architectural heritage.

DIŞ HATLAR GİDEN YOLCU
INTERNATIONAL DEPARTURES
istanbul

Heathrow West, Heathrow Airport

Hillingdon, London
Concept designed 2019

Designs for Heathrow West support the expansion of Heathrow Airport through the creation of a new Terminal 6 campus. The new terminal is connected to a satellite pier via a 300-metre-long passenger bridge that spans aircraft stands and the taxiway. The journey across the bridge will become an integral part of the arrival, departure and transfer journeys, offering a new passenger experience to those travelling through Heathrow. A fully automated/robotic baggage-handling system will connect to the existing Terminal 5 baggage-handling system, enabling both terminals to operate as a single hub.

From the upper level, passengers will experience the tree canopies and greenery of the levels below; all are brought together under an arching vault roof. The covered multimodal transport interchange incorporates a railway station, hotels and below-ground parking, allowing passengers to arrive safely and conveniently by train, bus, car or bicycle.

By facilitating seamless integration with public transportation systems, airports can significantly reduce their environmental impact, alleviate road congestion and enhance passenger mobility. The scheme offers innovative and robust solutions for this site, minimizing the land required while achieving the necessary hub capacity. Inherently flexible, it will enable the campus to adapt to changing passenger expectations over time.

The covered multimodal transport interchange includes a railway station, hotels and below-ground parking. Below: Elevation of the terminal and pier bridge.

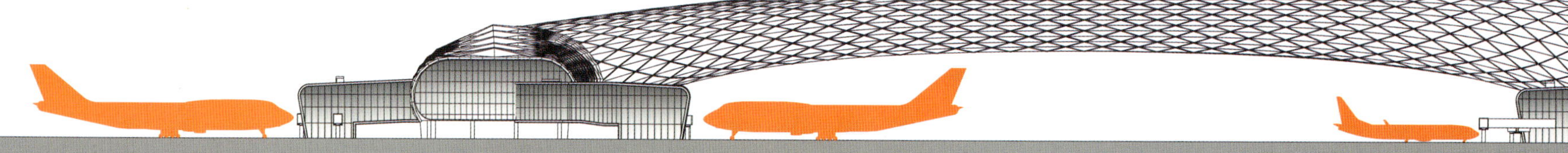

Overleaf: Scott Brownrigg is part of the team that has designed an alternative scheme for the Heathrow airport expansion, the new Terminal 6 campus.

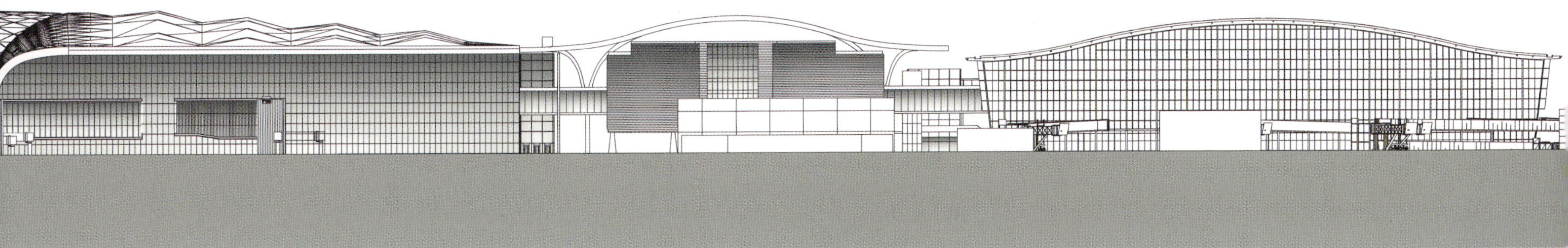

Future Thinking: Aviation

The aviation industry has long been a symbol of human progress, connecting places and cultures. However, this progress has come at a significant environmental cost, with aviation being a major contributor to greenhouse-gas emissions.
The first step towards a sustainable future involves re-evaluating and rethinking the design approach and consumption patterns. This means questioning choices and rules, challenging the necessity of energy-intensive design and considering the impact on the environment. The adoption of a holistic design approach creates opportunities to make more informed decisions that prioritize sustainability processes and eco-friendly alternatives.

The principles of 'the three R's – Rethink, Reduce and Reuse' have emerged as fundamental tenets of sustainable development. These three simple yet powerful words encapsulate a holistic approach to addressing some of the most pressing issues driving the future of terminal design. Designers must consider 'the three R's' in order to achieve significant reduction of carbon emissions and to collaborate on the target for a reduction in global warming. Perhaps the most significant aspect of rethinking sustainability in passenger-terminal design is a shift in mindset.

Examples of the ways in which passenger-terminal design can be redefined to help airports meet ambitious sustainability goals and carbon-reduction targets in line with international agreements include streamlining the journey and designing for the future.

Optimizing the footprint of a terminal can reduce walking distances for passengers, the need for mechanical transportation systems, and energy consumption. Up to 60 per cent of a building's embodied carbon is related to its structural material and foundations; reducing the overall footprint through the removal of non-essential facilities and possibly the baggage factory from the terminal building could create a reduction in embodied and operational carbon of around 30 per cent. Embracing natural ventilation is another means of reducing reliance on mechanical ventilation and, therefore, of reducing energy consumption associated with the operation of passenger-terminal buildings.

Designing terminals with flexibility in mind in order to accommodate future technological advancements and changes in passenger preferences is crucial to reduce the need for frequent renovations and associated resource consumption.

Replacing the baggage-handling system with luggage-delivery services is a radical idea that comes with challenges, but it presents an opportunity to significantly transform the airport operational and design paradigm. Meanwhile, rethinking the connectivity between future airport terminals and public transport through the creation of seamless multimodal interchanges can help to reduce environmental impact beyond the boundaries of an airport by providing passengers with ease of access via shared transportation.

Another key focus that is affecting the future of airport and terminal design is the challenge of delivering comfortable and pleasurable experiences for passengers and terminal users. A balance must be struck between standardization and personalization. Airports are dynamic spaces that cater for a wide array of passengers, from frequent business travellers to first-time tourists. Some passengers seek speed and efficiency, while others prioritize comfort or opportunities for relaxation.

Consistency in such elements as signage, wayfinding and efficient security protocols creates a reliable foundation, ensuring clarity and direction for all. At the same time, personalized services, such as lounges for business travellers and family areas for those with children, offer a tailored experience that meets individual preferences. Ensuring this balance will be key to future design work. The challenge lies in designing an environment that addresses the fundamental needs of all travellers – comfort, safety and ease of use – allowing flexibility and adaptability, while also offering a variety of choice to cater for all.

The practice's designs for the proposed new Terminal 6 at Heathrow Airport go beyond creating a facility that is fit for all, through the design of a multimodal transport interchange that will offer a sustainable way to serve the wider community.

Ultimately, the experience of a building or space is the result of how well physical, emotional and service-orientated factors are orchestrated. A well-designed space with wide corridors, high ceilings, natural light, good air quality and reduced noise, supported by thoughtful, clear wayfinding, excellent service and the incorporation of well-considered areas and details, can leave passengers feeling relaxed, satisfied and ready for their next journey.

Offices

Invigorating the workplace

Nick Ridout

Scott Brownrigg has been designing places for people to work throughout its history; in fact, the workplace has been one of the most prolific sectors the practice has been involved with. It was a series of architectural competition wins, including Westminster Bank in Haslemere and Haslemere Hall, that led Annesley Brownrigg to set up his own practice in 1910. Both buildings still stand and are operational today, with designs that reflect the tail end of the Arts and Crafts Movement in England.

Early commercial work tended to be located locally, either in Guildford or the surrounding areas. However, gradual growth from the mid-1950s allowed the practice to broaden its geographical presence, and by the mid-1960s it had offices and projects as far north as Scotland.

During this time and into the 1980s, much of the practice's work involved the refurbishment of existing office buildings deemed no longer fit for purpose. It would be another forty years or so before refurbishment and retrofit were widely adopted by the industry. Interestingly, the challenges associated with the retrofit of existing buildings, and fundamentally the approach to their subsequent upgrade, still resonate today.

Originally completed in 1934, Rennie House in Blackfriars, London, was constructed in reinforced concrete, 3 metres thick in some areas, with flat slab and mushroom-headed columns. When the practice

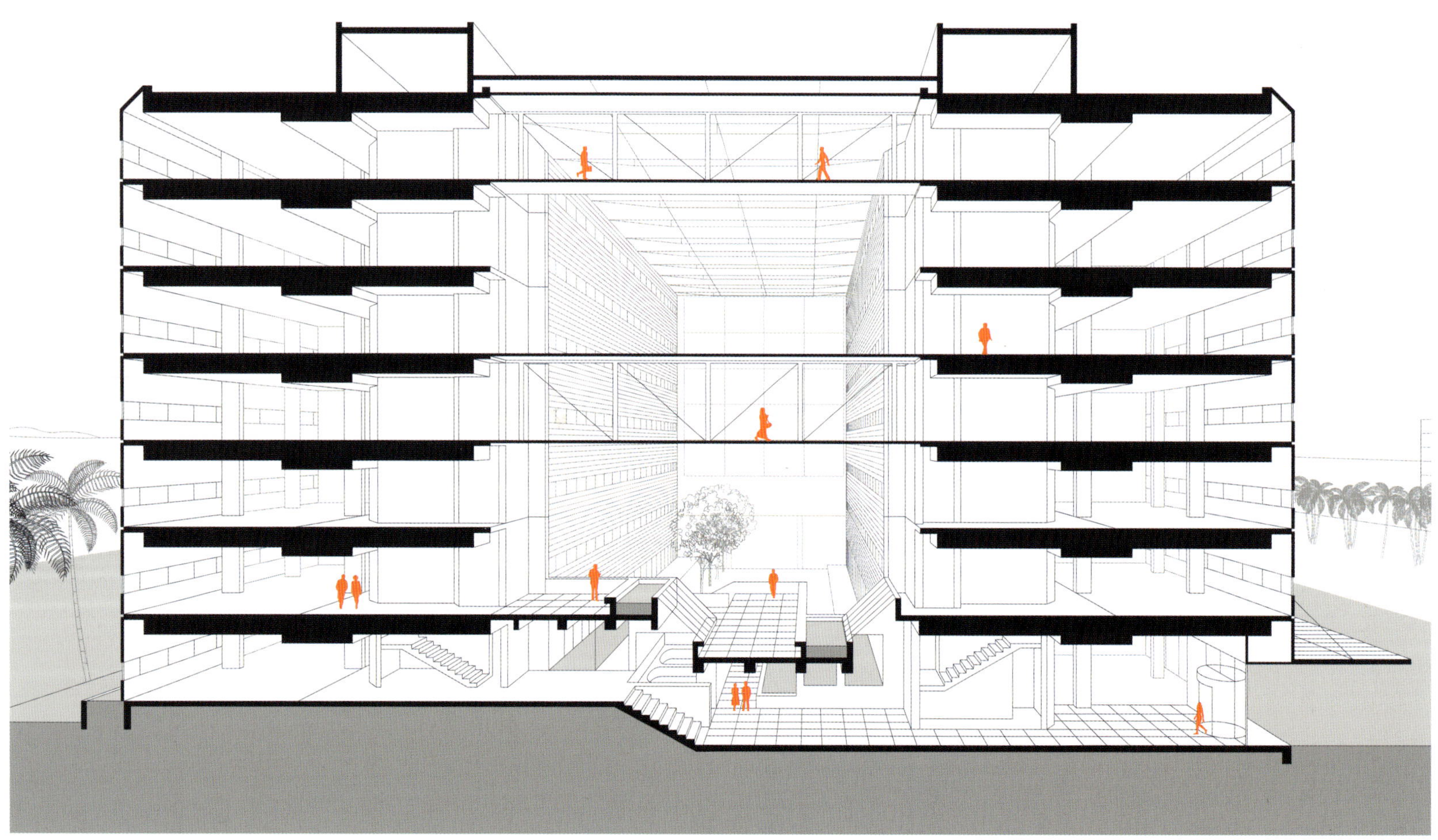

Abu Dhabi Trade Centre
Section through the Abu Dhabi Trade Centre, designed in 1976.

was appointed in 1975 to refurbish the factory building and repurpose it as an administrative office and laboratories for J. Sainsbury, works focused on improving the thermal efficiency of the building envelope and creating an open-plan floor space with amenity facilities that would appeal to staff and support well-being and productivity.

At the same time as work on Rennie House, the practice was designing the new-build offices in West Nile Street, Glasgow, for James Finlay & Co. – a contemporary building harmonious with the Victorian conservation area in which it was sited. Key elements of the design were heat recovery via light fittings set within bespoke coffered ceilings and solar-control double glazing to enhance user comfort and reduce energy consumption.

Extensive refurbishment projects continued throughout the 1970s, with the 'rehabilitation' for English Property Corporation of nearly half a block, fronting Long Acre and continuing into Floral Street, in the Covent Garden conservation area in London. The project consisted of existing Victorian and Edwardian office buildings, a solitary surviving Georgian townhouse and a builder's workshop. Work began on-site in 1976, and at the time the development was hailed as one of Covent Garden's most prestigious office blocks.

Expansion of the practice overseas during the 1970s led to a number of office-development opportunities, including, in 1976, the Abu Dhabi Trade Centre, a major city-centre project that incorporated 23,250 square metres of offices, a 7000-seat cinema, and retail for Sheikh Suroor bin Mohammed Al Nahyan; and, in 1978, the design

Victoria Gate
An innovative approach to development in the 1980s provided a robust framework for refurbishment as a modern, energy-efficient workspace in Woking in 2018.

for an administrative centre in Jubail, Saudi Arabia, for the Royal Commission for Jubail and Yanbu.

Recognition that the way people work inevitably changes over time has been a hallmark of the offices and places that Scott Brownrigg has designed and continues to design, coupled with a deep understanding of the commercial and financial drivers of its clients.

Victoria Gate (formerly known as Ryde House) in Woking, designed by a former chairman of Scott Brownrigg in the 1980s, was heralded for its design innovation at the time of its conception. It combined modernity and functional rationality, bringing energy measures to the exterior and using them in a deliberate way to articulate the facades. The scheme was future-proofed with a flexible internal layout and the ability to meet different servicing needs of future clients. On 6 June 1987, *Building Design* magazine commented: 'By ringing the building with a brise-soleil and placing the columns forward of the façade to support it, the architects have successfully enlivened what could otherwise have been just another uninteresting building.'

BBC White City
BBC White City in London was one of the practice's first major media projects, opening in 1990.

Aircraft-technology materials and bespoke integrated heating and cooling systems enabled a reduction in the thickness of the facade, which in turn supported an emerging 1.5-metre space-planning grid. This grid would both increase office space for the benefit of the tenant and maximize the lettable area for the developer.

In 2018 Scott Brownrigg was appointed by Aviva to redevelop and rebrand the building in order to facilitate a further increase in lettable space. The practice's proposal added 25 per cent net internal area to the footprint, achieved by stripping the design back to its frame and bringing the original 'out-board' external-column structure inside, creating an entirely new facade and interior and an additional fifth floor. Earning an Excellent rating for the environmental standard BREEAM, this transformation enabled it to become a high-specification building, with sixty secure cycle spaces, lockers, and new shower and changing facilities supporting the needs of a modern workforce, and flexible design principles ensuring its relevance far into the future.

In 1986 Scott Brownrigg & Turner, along with PE Consulting Services, wrote a report called 'Workplace 2000', which was published in both *The Times* and the *Daily Telegraph*. The report included thought-provoking and accurate insights into working in the year 2000 and beyond, with a focus on employee health and well-being and the provision of amenities to support them. Allowing staff to 'work from home' was recommended as being paramount to the financial success of a company. It took until 2020 before this notion became a material consideration.

The modern office is not a building but a machine for working in. Before long every single worker will be linked into a single integrated electronic network ... which needs to be designed into new intelligent buildings.

The report, together with a review of historic Scott Brownrigg schemes, underlines the fact that many of the design drivers used to help shape and define designs for office buildings today have been in existence for many years. The fundamentals of office design have remained true; there has been a shift of emphasis, rather than wholesale changes.

In the late 1980s, the practice designed one of its most recognizable projects, the administrative headquarters for the BBC at White City. White City had been the site of the 1908 Franco-British Exhibition and the White City Stadium, which was used for the 1908 Summer Olympics. The 46,500-square-metre, six-storey building was one of the first design-and-build contracts in the UK and was a game changer for the industry.

Ahead of its time in more ways than one, White City also provided an indication of the flexible and adaptable office buildings to come, with open-plan floor space, raised floors for cabling, false ceilings for lighting and air conditioning, and insulated metal partitions allowing for the reorganization of spaces as the needs of the BBC changed. The building also incorporated a state-of-the-art computerized building-management system at a cost of £1 million.

On the project's completion at the end of 1990, a headline in *The Guardian* read, 'It's a "fabulous piece of kit", but the BBC HQ represents a switch of power from architects to builder.' An envelope as big as St Paul's Cathedral was built and fully fitted out in just over two years, for £58 million, allowing the BBC to demonstrate extraordinary value at a time when the corporation was under immense scrutiny to provide value.

Following the rise in popularity of business parks between the mid-1980s and the year 2000, Scott Brownrigg developed a reputation as specialists in the field, designing and delivering individual buildings and wider masterplans for business parks throughout the UK.

The Oracle Corporation headquarters at Thames Valley Park completed in 1996, providing the technology firm with 23,000 square metres of prime office space. As one of the first buildings to incorporate vertically stacked plant, it was a project that would reappraise the requirements of office development. Avoiding the conventional solution of placing plant on the roof allowed the building to be serviced horizontally, thereby facilitating the creation of column-free space internally at the uppermost level. Fresh themes for integrated landscape and the showcasing of structural innovations – an approach that would be deployed across many of the practice's future office projects – earned accolades within architectural circles.

In 2000 the practice was appointed to design the new headquarters for the Environment Agency at Wallingford in Oxfordshire (pp. 52–55). The building was at the cutting edge of passive environmental design and, on completion in 2005, was a focal point of the annual British Council for Offices (BCO) conference.

500 Brook Drive (pp. 56–57) at Green Park is a highly flexible and adaptable building that won BCO Awards for the base build for the developer, PRUPIM, and for the tenant fit-out for Quintiles; both were designed by Scott Brownrigg.

Oracle Headquarters
Having reconfigured the masterplan at Thames Valley Park, Scott Brownrigg was appointed by Oracle Corporation UK Limited to design its headquarters, which completed in 1996.

In parallel to business parks, Scott Brownrigg continued to design and deliver new and refurbished urban office buildings for both developers and owner-occupiers. The acquisition of GMW in 2015 bolstered the practice's commercial work with a portfolio that included some of the most iconic modernist buildings in the City of London. The Commercial Union Tower, built in the late 1960s, was the tallest tower building in the City; it was also one of the first buildings in the UK to be built from the 'top down'. It was subsequently called the Aviva Tower and, in later years, St Helen's. GMW also designed 6–8 Bishopsgate, the headquarters of Barings Bank before its collapse in 1995.

In 1976 GMW completed 99 Bishopsgate, which for a while boasted the fastest lifts in Europe, travelling 6.5 metres per second. In 1993 the building was severely damaged by an IRA bomb, so GMW was once again appointed to work on the scheme, this time designing a significant refurbishment that entailed remodelling the main entrance and replacing the entire cladding system – just as had been done on the iconic Tower 42 building opposite.

In 1997 Scott Brownrigg converted the former Lonrho headquarters into 6500 square metres of speculative office space over eight floors at Cheapside House. In 2008 it was commissioned to design Eden House, a new five-storey office building in the Spitalfields Market Development Area for Royal London Asset Management. Since then, the practice has maintained a consistent presence in the City of London.

The refurbishment and extension of 41 Lothbury in 2014 brought a new lease of life to a traditional City landmark, increasing workspace through the addition of contemporary office floors and the restoration of – to paraphrase Peter Rees, City Planning Officer for the City of London – 'the

The Quadrant, Network Rail National Centre
The Cat. A design and fit-out of Network Rail's National Centre in Milton Keynes consolidates 3000 staff from various UK offices into a single location.

best banking hall in London'. As a result, the practice facilitated a 30 per cent increase in net internal area in a Grade II*-listed building.

Work on 67 Lombard Street (completed 2014) and 28 Chancery Lane (completed 2016) offered many similarities, with the retention of historic facades in both schemes and the addition of a contemporary floor above. Flexible and adaptable floor plates facilitate significant gains in net internal area and respond to fast-changing occupier profiles in the City, increasing building life and ensuring relevance far into the future.

A different approach was adopted for the refurbishment for Network Rail of Puddle Dock, a 1960s building located on the riverside in Blackfriars. Reglazing and the careful distribution of MEP services allowed a low-cost, high-impact refurbishment of the building in 2017.

In 2019 the practice was commissioned to refurbish the Grade II-listed Adelaide House on London Bridge. Adelaide House was London's first steel-frame building, and at the time of construction in 1924 was one of the tallest buildings in the city, second only to St Paul's Cathedral. The refurbishment brings the historic building into the twenty-first century with a contemporary workspace. A key feature is a new roof terrace with sweeping views of the Thames and a rooftop pavilion, restoring the essence behind the original design, which boasted its own rooftop putting green and gardens.

While much of Scott Brownrigg's historic work has been with developers and funds, more recently owner-occupier buildings have provided a rich breadth and depth of work for the practice, often including both the building design and the interior fit-out. One such example is the impressive headquarters building for Arm (pp. 60–63) at Peterhouse Technology Park in Cambridge, which has been holistically designed and fitted out to cater for a particular neurodiverse population. The highly flexible design can be extended or split simply in a way that supports expansion, contraction or subletting in the future.

The Quadrant in Milton Keynes for Network Rail (completed 2012) was conceived as a series of neighbourhoods off a central 'street', designed to encourage interaction between employees. Unusually, a 15-metre-wide floor plate was adopted to provide the required floor space while also allowing for natural ventilation, saving the client both cost and time. The scheme won a BCO Regional Award.

Completed in 2017, the 10,500-square-metre Tamesis building provided a new workspace for Royal London and its tenant Gartner in Egham, Surrey. While this was a traditional arrangement with a landlord and a tenant, both agreed that the benefits of a close, collaborative relationship with each other and with their design teams, namely Scott Brownrigg, would help the project. The building introduced well-being and amenity, with collaboration at its heart. Though catering to Gartner's specific requirements, the base build and fit-out were designed to be universally lettable. A 'long life, loose fit' philosophy led to the building being raised above the ground in order to retain the original flood capacity and allow local flood waters to run beneath.

The practice's work for the international not-for-profit organization CABI in Wallingford (pp. 64–65) replaced an old school building occupied by CABI for more than thirty-three years with a two-storey, low-carbon headquarters that integrates an experimental biodiverse landscape with a new collaborative flexible working environment. Situated in an Area of Outstanding Natural Beauty, the building responds to its surroundings with a living roof, which will attract insects and birds and enhance biodiversity.

Red Kite House

Wallingford, Oxfordshire
Completed 2005

Red Kite House is a 2800-square-metre office designed for the Environment Agency. On completion in 2005, it was considered to be at the forefront of sustainable office design, and it set the standard for the practice's ongoing sustainable-design work.

The project was designed to achieve a BREEAM Excellent rating, with carbon emissions 26 per cent below the Department of the Environment's *Energy Efficiency in Offices* guidance figures. The design was developed specifically to allow for environmental factors, with each element performing a function either to passively cool the building or to reduce energy consumption.

Notably, the project challenged the institutional norm of a 'four-pipe fan-coil' approach to cooling, with wind turbines integrated on the roof to support natural ventilation via automatic openable windows. It was the first office building in the UK to use turbines for this purpose.

Red Kite House won or was shortlisted for a number of sustainability awards, including the RICS Southeast Regional Sustainability Award in 2006 and the Civic Trust Sustainability Award in 2007, and in 2011 it featured on the front cover of the government's *Low Carbon Construction Action Plan*.

The building is curved in plan and is orientated east–west in order to capture prevailing wind for natural ventilation. Below: Section through the building, showing the sustainable-design features.

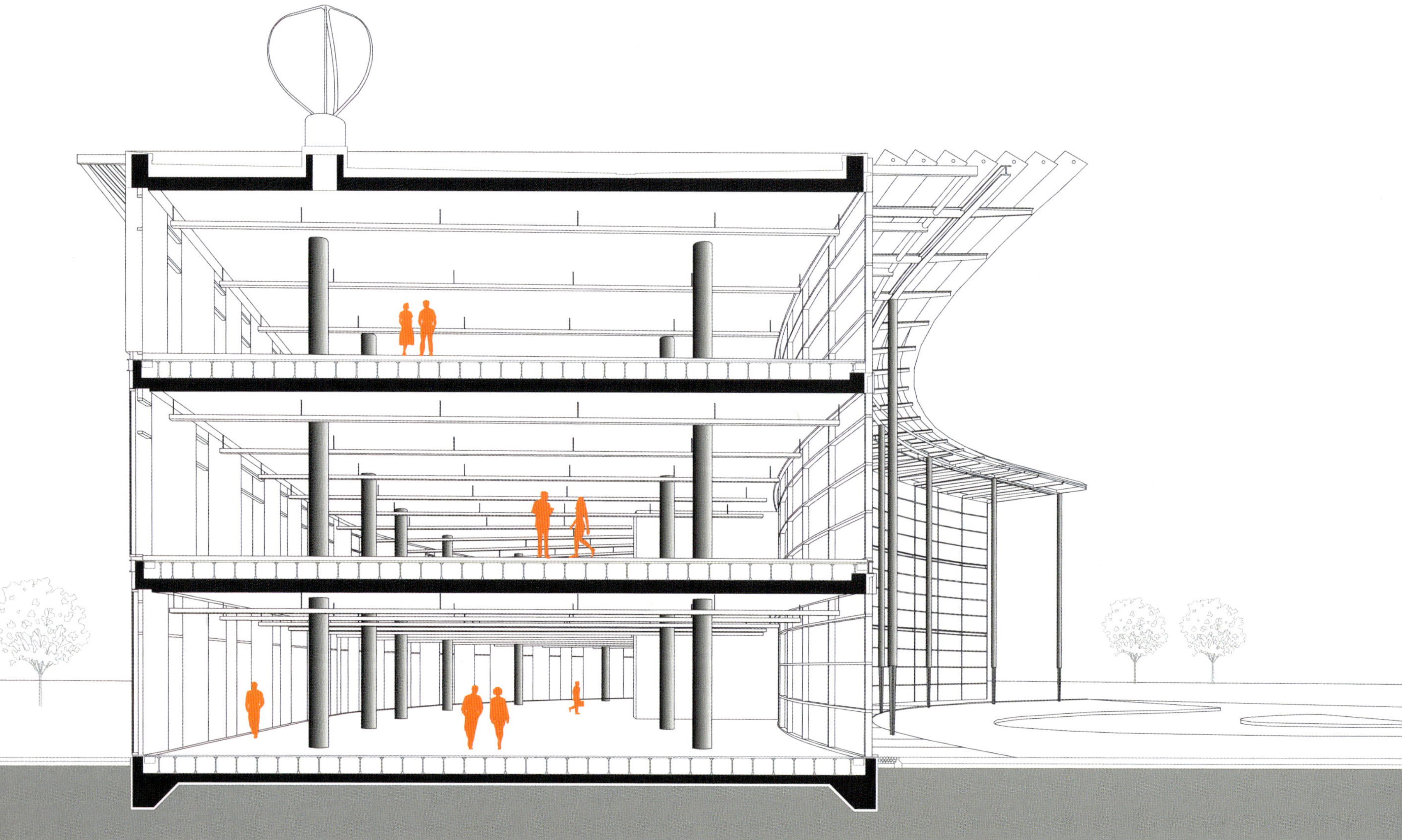

Red Kite House
Photovoltaic cells on the south-facing brise-soleil provide the interior with shade and generate approximately 20 per cent of the building's electrical power.

500 Brook Drive

Reading, Berkshire
Completed 2009

Located on a business park on the outer edge of Reading, 500 Brook Drive is a five-storey headquarters building that provides over 13,000 square metres of office space for a leading pharmaceutical brand. The futuristic design was developed to the highest standards of occupier comfort, energy efficiency and environmental amenity, and with flexibility in mind.

The bold sculpted design wraps around a full-height central atrium that is shaded by an oversailing roof and flanked by two opaque glass-clad stair towers. Cantilevered bridges connect the two wings on the upper levels. Two sculptural external staircases are unique in their integral structural support, using an inner string cut from a single steel tube to emulate the form of a helix ribbon.

A reduced dependency on cars is encouraged through higher-than-standard cycle and changing provision and access to a comprehensive network of cycle routes, combined with incorporation of the building into Green Park's established green travel plan.

A BREEAM Excellent rating was achieved through active displacement floor ventilation and passive chilled beams, which create a healthier working environment. As a result, the project won the BCO Regional Commercial Workplace Award in 2010 and the BCO Regional Fit Out of Workplace Award in 2012.

The brief was to create a statement building that would have presence and reinforce the tenant's position as a leading global pharmaceutical company.

BP Sunbury

Sunbury-on-Thames, Surrey
Completed 2015

Completed in 2015, this 9350-square-metre, four-storey office building is the final masterplan element of the eastern side of BP's International Centre for Business and Technology in Sunbury-on-Thames. The scheme integrates with existing offices and forms a harmonious connection with the other buildings and with local context and community.

Scott Brownrigg's architecture and interior design teams created an adaptable design that is suitable for the future needs of the global corporation. The building was designed from the inside out following a comprehensive workplace strategy, and reflects BP's core brand values and work patterns, providing a modern, vibrant and energizing space with a variety of work settings that enhance collaborative working and effectiveness.

The envelope design features passive sustainable-design measures through the building orientation and the way the floor plates and atria have been arranged. Dichroic glass fins respond to different daylight conditions, helping to minimize heat gain and maximize daylight penetration, alongside low-energy smart building services and controls.

The design incorporates a variety of work settings into the building to provide choice, support collaborative working and enhance productivity.

Arm Headquarters

Cambridge
Completed 2019

On completion in 2019, the Arm headquarters was the first major new office building on Peterhouse Technology Park (pp. 114–15) in twenty years. Tailored to Arm's identity as the world's leading semiconductor technology designer, the building and interior design were inspired by the structure of silicon, which underlies semiconductor technology. The lattice-like crystalline theme permeates every element of the building's design, from the facade down to the smallest design detail.

Scott Brownrigg worked closely with the occupants throughout the design process to ensure that Arm's brand values were reflected in the project. As a result, the design ensures that conversation and collaboration are celebrated and encouraged; atrium spaces unite teams of people, driving discussions and ingenuity.

Arm had never previously enjoyed the luxury of large public volumes, so these spaces were a key driver for the client. The column-free atrium can support large drop-down screens so that all employees can be brought together, under one roof, in Cambridge. By repeating the silicon structure throughout the external and internal design, the completed building provides employees with not only an inspirational working environment, but also a strong sense of place and identity, reflecting Arm's global role and legacy in the development of integrated-circuit technology.

The building achieved a BREEAM Excellent rating, with bespoke 'crystalline' fins providing solar shading and relief to the facades that sit above the transparent and permeable glazing on the ground floor. Provision of flexible services, alongside the ability to subdivide each floor or extend tenancies horizontally and vertically, future-proofs the design by creating a profitable asset for the landlord and a great workplace for tenants.

The opportunity to work closely with an innovative client enabled the creation of a truly unique project, one that embodies the goals, aspirations and needs of Arm and reflects its very DNA. The distinctive nature of Arm's business has been captured in the fabric of the architecture, the cellular nature of teams and neighbourhoods, and the collaborative heart of the project. Wrapped in, protected by and permeated with silicon-crystal references, this project delivers standards typical of City of London offices to Cambridge, providing a one-of-a-kind workplace to support one of the UK's true technological success stories.

Facilitating the consolidation of offices around Cambridge, Arm's headquarters building is designed to accommodate 1700 employees and to support the firm's continued growth within the technology sector. Below: Section through the building.

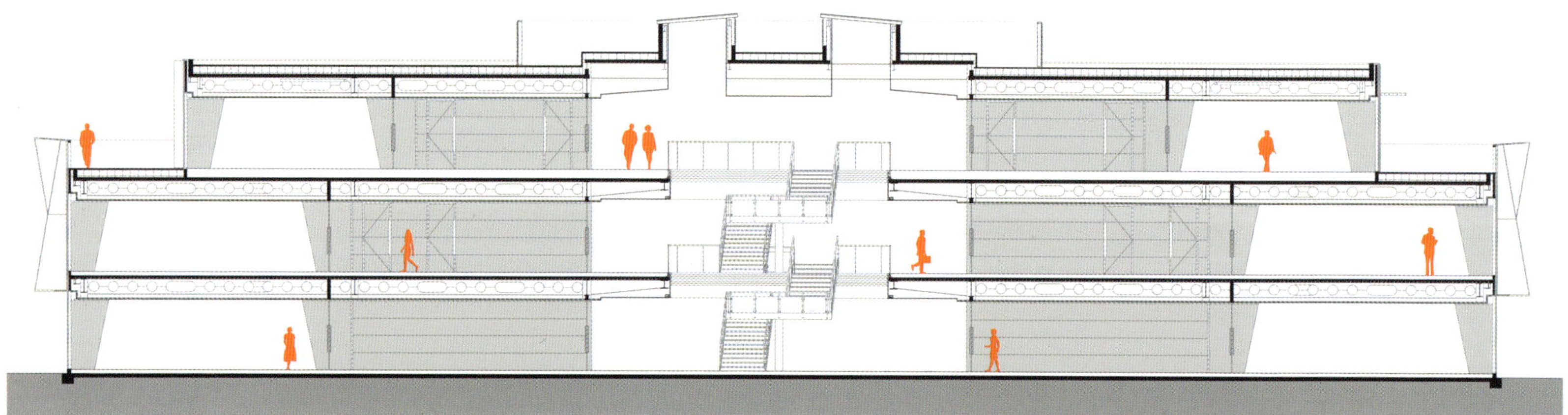

Arm Headquarters
Varied settings at Arm's co-working space in Cambridge create visual interest while supporting the changing requirements and emotional well-being of teams.

CABI Headquarters

Wallingford,
Oxfordshire
Completed 2020

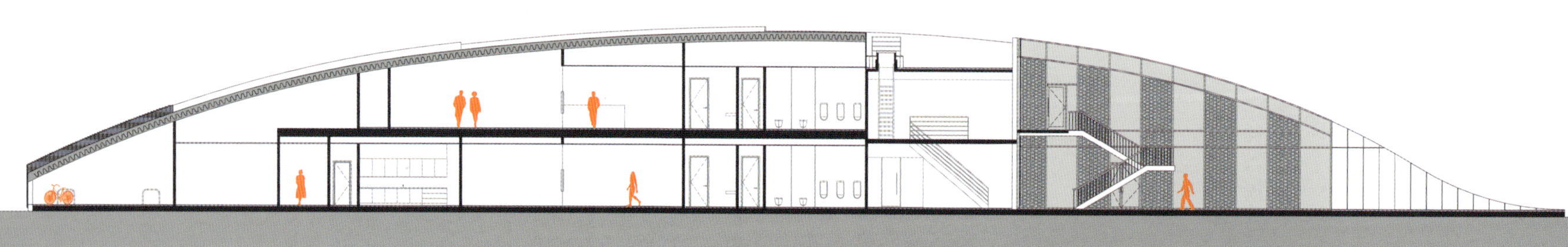

Situated in an Area of Outstanding Natural Beauty in Oxfordshire, this purpose-built headquarters embodies not-for-profit CABI's mission through a low-carbon design set within an experimental biodiverse landscape.

The project is characterized by a curvilinear living roof designed to attract insects and birds and to integrate the two-storey building into its surroundings. Inside, the collaborative, flexible working environment accommodates up to 180 members of staff, who are provided with a range of amenities, including a cafe-restaurant, meeting rooms and a conference room/auditorium.

The design harnesses a fabric-first approach and passive sustainability principles to provide a comfortable, low-carbon design in operation. Particular focus was placed on the provision of natural ventilation; this was achieved through an innovative perforated facade that permits cool air into the building and ensures a continual flow of clean air throughout the day and night. Foreshadowing challenges to come, this focus on air quality ensured that the building was well equipped to suit the health and well-being needs of office users during the Covid-19 pandemic.

An innovative traffic-light system is used to reduce reliance on mechanical and electrical systems, prompting occupants to open windows to maintain a natural, healthy and comfortable working environment. Opposite, bottom: Section through the building.

Future Thinking: Offices

As hybrid and flexible ways of working become ever more prevalent, accelerated by the Covid-19 pandemic, offices must work harder to help attract and retain talent, and to encourage people to leave their homes and commute to work. Therefore, the workplace needs to offer functions that cannot be replicated remotely: the opportunity to meet and socialize with colleagues, to collaborate and to feel part of a community.

With reduced office occupancy comes reduced footfall in towns and cities, which has had a devastating effect on the high street. During the pandemic, the practice presented ideas to the City of London on how the high street could be brought back to life, using Cheapside – which is generally treated as a route rather than a destination – as an example. The vision was for an 'urban park' that would connect the gardens surrounding St Paul's Cathedral with the Bank of England and provide a setting for educational engagement against a backdrop of cafes, restaurants and sports facilities, all combining to create a unique new destination with vitality along Cheapside. The repurposing of spaces and the introduction of a range of diverse uses offer great potential to bring a sense of vibrancy and community back to these streets.

The oncoming effect of artificial intelligence will no doubt further alter the way people work. How this develops is still to be seen, but the thinking is that tasks considered more mundane and repetitive will become increasingly automated, resulting in more time for conceptualizing and interacting with fellow workers, and less time spent sitting at a desk performing individual tasks. The emphasis on personal interaction will grow, making the office more of a place in which to socialize rather than to focus.

Leases are becoming more short-term and flexible as companies face an uncertain future, so buildings must be designed to flex as much as possible and adapt to allow tenants to expand or contract as required. Part of Scott Brownrigg's recent research, the Adaptable Base Build Concept, addresses this situation. The office building is conceived as a three-dimensional object that can quickly, simply and cheaply be adapted to allow floors to interlink vertically as well as horizontally, providing tenants with the potential to expand up and down as well as laterally, with MEP services configured to support this adaptation.

Sustainability plays an increasingly prominent role as the climate crisis evolves. Another key piece of the practice's research is the Timber Office Concept with Stora Enso – a modular timber office concept. An advantage of office buildings constructed in wood – in addition to the environmental and efficiency benefits associated with building with timber – is that they can enhance occupant health and well-being. Recent studies indicate that natural design in the workplace can increase employee health and well-being by 13 per cent and productivity by 8 per cent.

The Timber Office combines carbon reduction in building fabric and innovation with an adaptable design that uses a modular, kit-of-parts approach.

The system is comparable to steel and concrete, but it has all the advantages of a timber product, including reduced construction time, reduced carbon and transport emissions, and improved life-cycle performance.

While these concepts offer a viable solution to new-build offices, the true future for office buildings is retrofit, particularly in urban environments.

Current planning legislation places emphasis on the retention of building fabric and, where necessary, a strong justification for demolition and rebuild. Buildings constructed in the early 2000s are coming to the end of their lease cycles, and such buildings tend to have the right structural and spatial qualities to suit retrofit. MEP can be simply updated and technology integrated to create a smart building that reacts to users' requirements.

Understanding and learning how to truly cater for a neurodiverse population is a focus of Scott Brownrigg's current and future projects. Provision of a variety of highly adaptable spaces, with consideration given to such elements as colour, sound, smell and temperature, allows people to customize spaces to suit their own needs or those of a particular group.

The 'long life, loose fit' mantra will become increasingly relevant as emphasis grows on carbon-saving and the retention of fabric, and as offices are expected to accommodate a widening variety of uses. It may be that architects need to find alternative uses for office buildings altogether as the existing stock reaches the end of its current life cycle and the way people work continues to change over time.

Interior Design

Creating engaging internal environments

Beatriz Gonzalez

Scott Brownrigg's history of providing interior design spans both private and public sectors, from offices, residential and hospitality through to education, defence and transport. Such diversity has allowed the practice to cross-fertilize ideas and blur the boundaries between qualities that make a great workplace, learning, hospitality or living environment. What ties these together is the company's passion for great design and the desire to push creatively in order to impact everyday lives positively.

The year 2024 marked the twenty-fifth anniversary of the practice's providing a dedicated workplace interiors service – an embedded service to deliver a specific offer to clients, rather than a supplementary addition to its recognized architectural offering.

While working with big corporate end-user companies in the 1990s, the practice recognized a need to develop a specialism beyond simple Cat. A work: to provide bespoke interiors catering to the needs of a business and reflective of its personality, brand, ambitions and growth plans. As a result, a specialist interiors team was created within Scott Brownrigg with the skills and expertise to offer clients an optimum bespoke service. The team's work initially concentrated on receptions and front-of-house areas – spaces that created the first impression of a company. This quickly developed into encompassing all areas of a building, with a growing remit that included evaluating existing internal spaces and significantly improving and optimizing working environments; analysing and exploring spaces that would best reflect how employees could work and aligning these to a client's vision and goals.

Eastern Electricity in 1993 was one of the first major corporations that trusted Scott Brownrigg to evaluate its business, deliver its buildings and review its internal-space requirements. It was from this point that the practice's client list rapidly grew.

In 2002 Scott Brownrigg completed the six-building campus for T-Mobile at Hatfield Business Park, with architecture and interior design services carried out consecutively and delivered in just two and a half years owing to the fast-track nature of the design-and-build contract.

The year 2011 was exceptional for the interior design offering at the practice, bringing a significant number of developments and successes: the expansion of its corporate-client list and an impressive portfolio of design work for Google, Centrica, Bain & Company, Quintiles, Chartis Insurance, Baker McKenzie, Eli Lilly, Celgene, Otkritie Bank, Cisco, Boeing, Almacantar, Land Securities, The Office Group and GVA, to name just a few. The team was invited to compete for, and subsequently won, numerous high-profile appointments from leading corporate businesses to design their offices, and from leading property companies to design and refresh buildings. During this time, the practice was growing internationally, with studios opening in Abu Dhabi, Croatia and Moscow to support its design work in Europe and the Middle East.

There was also a significant shift in the services offered by the interiors team from this period onwards, with the provision of not just interior design but also workplace consulting services; Scott Brownrigg worked with Celgene, Centrica and Eli Lilly on their workplace strategies. This approach was taken further in 2015, when the practice designed a building 'from the inside out' for BP at its International Centre for Business and Technology in Sunbury-on-Thames. The design for the building's interiors informed its architectural design following a comprehensive workplace strategy that reflected the client's brand values and work patterns. Creating a series of vibrant and energizing spaces, a variety of work settings are incorporated into the four-storey building in order to support collaborative working.

The practice's expertise in this area was reinforced in 2017, when it created a dedicated workplace strategy service, Design Strategy Unit, which went on to partner with the workplace specialists IPWC in 2020. Design Strategy Unit was born out of the need to offer clients a continuity of service by providing engagement, analysis and workplace strategy in parallel with test fits and interior design. The successful launch of the unit at the Worktech conference in 2017 was accompanied by the development of a digital interactive tool, the Workstyle Profiler.

The interiors team has a vision to create sustainable, user-centric and data-driven workplace environments that cater to the dynamic needs of a diverse workforce by focusing on user experience, quality of product and delivery. The team has a track record in delivering purposeful, high-quality workplaces for such clients as Expedia, NBCUniversal, Thomson Reuters, Reckitt

Reckitt Benckiser Science and Innovation Centre
The retrofitted Reckitt Benckiser Science and Innovation Centre in Hull comprises modern workspaces, R&D facilities and collaborative areas, driving forward the latest discoveries in consumer health.

Benckiser, London Stock Exchange Group (LSEG), NCR, Lloyds Banking Group, Arm, State Street, Chaucer Insurance, Roshn, Volkswagen and G-Research.

An important element of Scott Brownrigg's interiors offering has been the ability to understand a corporate business, interpret its brand and implement new ways of working that can be rolled out to other locations. In 2008 the practice started working for Arlington Securities (now Goodman) on its London headquarters at 10 Old Burlington Street. The brief was to create a spatial brand identity that could be implemented at numerous locations, including the Theale HQ in Reading and the Goodman Amsterdam office.

In 2017 the practice worked with the travel technology company Expedia (pp. 82–83), initially producing the company's global workplace guidelines, then designing its offices in Hamburg, Jordan, Dubai and Munich. The collaboration culminated in the commission of Expedia's 22,000-square-metre EMEA headquarters in the Angel Building, London.

A long-standing relationship with Thomson Reuters – first on its Vintners Place offices in 2011, followed by its 46,450-square-metre European Hub Headquarters at 5 Canada Square, Canary Wharf, which completed in 2020 (pp. 88–89) – led to the practice creating a set of global design standards to be used for all the company's future work implemented in other offices across its portfolio. The practice was also involved, from the early stages, in the design of the Thomson Reuters offices in Times Square, New York, and Stamford, Connecticut. The office fit-out in Canary Wharf was, at the time, London's largest agile working environment. The design aimed to establish a cultural landmark for employees, prioritizing circularity and innovative, flexible work settings. The successful delivery of the project strengthened the relationship with the client, which continued with a subsequent phase for its subsidiary Refinitiv, now LSEG. The practice designed additional offices for LSEG in its headquarters in Paternoster Square, as well as in Amsterdam, Nottingham and Gdynia, Poland. Scott Brownrigg also developed LSEG's global design guidelines. The locations of its strategic global hubs have enabled the practice to support its clients worldwide, from Europe to the Middle East and the United States.

In 2020 Scott Brownrigg completed its largest fit-out outside the UK, for NCR, delivering the American fintech firm's international hub in Belgrade, Serbia. This project encompassed over 30,000 square metres of office space, including a customer-experience centre. In the same year, the team secured the design for Roshn's offices in Riyadh, Saudi Arabia. Today the project is regarded as one of the region's top office fit-outs.

The current notions of 'plug and play' and the circular economy are not new to the practice's interiors offering. In 2011 its designs for Google (pp. 76–77) at 123 Buckingham Palace Road, London, needed to accommodate over 600 employees, surprisingly with desks for all. Of significance was the fact that all the interiors were required to be 'non-fixed' and easy to dismantle. The project pushed the boundaries of fun design and creativity.

Scott Brownrigg's well-established relationship with Thomson Reuters enabled the significant reuse of materials at Canada Square, including the raised access floor, ceiling tiles, demountable glazed partitions and 50 per cent of the furniture; the existing lighting was repurposed as LED.
At the LSEG offices in Paternoster Square, the application of key lessons and circular design principles created a fully flexible, adaptable space that anticipates future needs. Instead of traditional cellular spaces, modular furniture pods were designed, while other features that support disassembly and reuse were created. For example, timber flooring was installed using magnetic fixings for easy removal and reuse, and wall finishes were applied with dry-fix solutions to facilitate future adaptations. Such sustainable practices

have become integral to Scott Brownrigg's design process across all its interiors projects, reflecting the practice's commitment to environmental responsibility.

Over the years, Scott Brownrigg's interior design offering has breathed new life into stunning listed buildings, and has always been respectful of their heritage while ensuring the provision of twenty-first-century design standards and working environments. Projects of note include the Grade II-listed 25 Berkeley Square, an impressive 1920s building that was the former headquarters of Cadbury. The fit-out in the same building for the chocolate brand Green & Black's completed in the same year, 2009. The refurbishment in 2011 of Grade II-listed Green Park House, 15 Stratton Street in Mayfair – originally built as an Arts and Crafts residence – converted the six-storey building into serviced offices. Similarly, in 2009, the refurbishment of Warnford Court in the City, constructed in 1884 and originally the back office of the Bank of England, ensured that the building could continue to be let to multiple occupiers while work on the 100 individual suites was carried out. In 2019 the practice was commissioned to refurbish the Grade II-listed Adelaide House on London Bridge.

Scott Brownrigg has won many awards for its interiors work. In 2012 Quintiles (pp. 78–79) at 500 Brook Drive won the BCO Regional Fit Out of Workplace Award, two years after the same project won the BCO Regional Award for the base build. In 2014 the design for Arthur J. Gallagher in the Walbrook Building (pp. 80–81) won the BCO Regional Fit Out of Workplace Award and subsequently the BCO National Award.

Such success has continued throughout the last decade, with BCO Regional Awards for VW Financial Services in Milton Keynes in 2016 (Fit Out); Tamesis in Egham, for Gartner, in 2018 (Corporate Workplace); Victoria Gate, Woking, in 2019 (Refurbished/Recycled Workplace); Reckitt Benckiser, Hull, in 2020 (Refurbished/Recycled Workplace); and CABI Headquarters, Wallingford, in 2023 (Corporate Workplace).

A commitment to well-being, employee experience and inclusivity has enabled the practice to gain a deep understanding of the people it designs for. It creates environments where employees can truly thrive, and where the varied needs of users are prioritized. Most recently, the

Tamesis, Gartner Headquarters
The fit-out of the European headquarters for Gartner in Egham, Surrey, creates an environment befitting a global technology company and delivers immediate impact on arrival.

design of offices that cater for a significant number of neurodivergent employees has involved the carefully consideration of unique requirements.

During the design of Arm's headquarters in Cambridge (pp. 60–63), the emphasis was on creating dedicated spaces for project-focused work in order to enhance individual concentration, while collaboration areas were centred around a 'central street'. A variety of spaces was essential to accommodate different users and purposes, from private areas for individual or team focus to lively, open collaboration zones.

At G-Research's office in Soho (completed 2024), Scott Brownrigg designed an Immersive Tuneable Hub, where employees can personalize their environment, adjusting sound, lighting, colour and visual graphics to suit their preferences. This bespoke, user-centric approach is what makes each of the practice's designs unique.

While workplace design has remained a core area of expertise for the practice's interiors offering throughout its history, the design of world-class hospitality interiors has been equally important. Scott Brownrigg's hospitality designs have encompassed well-known global brands, the refurbishment of landmark buildings and the interior design of new builds.

When the Grade II-listed Westminster County Court building in St Martin's Lane, London, was transformed into the flagship Browns restaurant in 1997, the practice was responsible for its interior design. The project provided a new lease of life for the landmark building, successfully retaining its unique character while converting it for other functional use.

In 2004 the redevelopment of the historic Free Trade Hall, one of Manchester's most well-known and treasured landmarks, into the luxury Radisson

Hyatt Regency London Stratford
Brass light fittings, marble fixtures, luxury velvet furnishings and jewel colours offer a contemporary take on the glamour and travel of the 1920s.

Edwardian Hotel combined the Grade II*-listed facade with a new sixteen-storey tower connected by a glazed atrium. Artefacts retrieved from the original building remained on display. This project led to work on the Radisson Blu Waterfront Hotel in St Helier, Jersey, with an impressive interior design inspired by the coastal views. Other recent hotels have included the Assembly Hotel, Leicester Square, which has a design informed by famous alumni of Central Saint Martins college – Stella McCartney, Gareth Pugh and Alexander McQueen – and the 172-room Hilton Terrace Mount in Bournemouth, designed in collaboration with the fashion brand Ted Baker.

With an established reputation for hotel refurbishment and interiors work, Scott Brownrigg secured a commission by the iconic brand Hard Rock following the transformation of the Cumberland Hotel in Marble Arch into the Hard Rock Hotel London (pp. 84–87). The practice was responsible for designing the main reception, the VIP reception and all the public spaces, including two vibrant bars, the Hard Rock Cafe and the Hard Rock Shop. Reflecting the brand and the city's rock heritage, displays of memorabilia throughout the hotel's public areas narrated the story of London's musical artists. Among the music-related features was a drumstick installation above the reception, the striking central Lobby Bar, and a mirrored ceiling in the Rock Royalty Lounge, where the acoustics were designed to facilitate live music performances. The hotel opened in 2019.

More recent refurbishments include, in 2022, the Hyatt Regency and Hyatt House hotels in Stratford, London, converted from Holiday Inns. Their interior designs reflect the connectivity of Stratford, with subtle nods to the Victorian Golden Age of train travel and Art Deco influences.

Scott Brownrigg's designs for hospitality extend overseas. Historically, Cyprus has provided an array of hospitality and residential opportunities for the practice. Of note was the provision of architecture, masterplanning and interior design services for the five-star Elysium Beach Resort in Paphos. Completed in 2002, it was named by the *Sunday Times* as the 'Best [New] Resort Hotel in the World'. In 2009 the practice completed the refurbishment of the five-star Amathus Beach Hotel in Limassol, originally designed in the 1960s by Walter Gropius. The project involved extensive changes to the facade, interior and terrace spaces.

Scott Brownrigg continues to embrace the challenge of understanding the business, culture, brand and customers of its clients as much as the aesthetic principles of great design based on the use of lighting, textures, colour, spatial sensations, materials and sounds. Listening to the client and reviewing all ideas, the practice brings fresh vision and imagination to all its projects. Its boutique service is powered by the drive to make things better by creating adaptive, inclusive and inspiring spaces, tailored to a client's needs. Client-centric and data-driven, the practice continually explores new working strategies to pave the way for future generations.

Hard Rock Hotel London
The Hard Rock Hotel London was home to displays of memorabilia celebrating the music legends who stayed at the Marble Arch location.

Google

Westminster, London
Completed 2011

To accommodate a growing workforce, Scott Brownrigg supported Google with the fit-out of a state-of-the-art 7700-square-metre workspace in Victoria featuring a new reception area and a range of individual work and collaboration spaces and health and leisure amenities, including a sushi bar. While the look, feel and branding were distinctly Google, a local London–Brighton theme set the office apart, incorporating many iconic elements and 3D graphic artwork to reinforce wayfinding and enhance visitor experience. Adaptability was built into the space-planning and workplace strategy to allow for future growth. A loose-fit design solution with the specification of high-quality furniture provided flexibility to move and reuse elements of the design at the end of the lease. Keen to push new boundaries in the way that its staff work, Google was among the first companies to adopt hot-desking, providing collaborative spaces where employees could 'touch down' with their laptops.

A combination of unique work settings and well-being facilities – including restaurants, a yoga studio and a massage and spa treatment centre – helped to make Google one of the most sought-after places to work. The project is a good example of Scott Brownrigg's design philosophy at the time – one that focused on the 'in-between spaces'.

Brightly coloured timber beach-hut meeting rooms, original dodgem cars and traditional red telephone booths provided a range of quirky workspaces that reinforced the quintessentially British theme throughout.

Quintiles

Reading, Berkshire
Completed 2011

The Quintiles European headquarters was formerly located at Scott Brownrigg-designed 500 Brook Drive in Reading (pp. 56–57). Representing a change in workplace strategy for the organization, the fit-out was designed to deliver a dynamic and flexible working environment, future-proofed to accommodate headcount growth.

Fundamental to the design concept was the delivery of a more open-plan environment with improved natural light and access to collaborative areas to increase staff welfare and productivity. A mix of permanent offices, hot-desking and open-plan spaces facilitated a more collaborative working approach while helping to maintain the confidentiality of various projects for different customers. The workspaces were supported by a range of amenity and welfare spaces, including a business lounge, a restaurant and world-class training facilities for both customers and employees.

Careful thought and attention to detail resulted in a workplace designed for optimal productivity, enabling colleagues to meet the changing needs and challenges of Quintiles's business. The technologically advanced single site was a big step forward for Quintiles, expediting an even higher level of collaboration and effectiveness between teams to better serve their biopharmaceutical customers.

Providing employees with the opportunity to help make decisions during the design process was key in generating an inherent sense of ownership and pride in the new workspace.

The project was one of few to win a BCO Award for the base build (2010) and for the fit-out (2012), both of which were designed by Scott Brownrigg.

Arthur J. Gallagher

City of London
Completed 2013

Arthur J. Gallagher consolidated 640 employees from three locations into a single new headquarters in the Walbrook Building, taking the basement, ground, first and seventh floors. After winning the commission via a design competition, Scott Brownrigg created a vibrant, inspiring internal environment – one that promotes greater collaboration and new ways of working, supports future growth plans and delivers a world-class client experience. It was a major challenge to bring life and light into the existing deep floor plans. The ground floor needed to provide a reception, space for 150 staff, a broker's lounge, meeting rooms and other facilities. The inward-sloping facade on the seventh floor produced a number of challenges. Two oculus-shaped atria served as the inspiration for the design, offering the opportunity to create something truly unique. The ground-floor oculus room, with its sloping, blue-tinted glazed walls, mirrors the location, shape and size of the atrium on the floor above, creating the illusion that the upper atrium extends down through the ground-floor ceiling.

The seventh-floor radial space-planning responds to the base build and the atria, maximizing floor space and creating a range of settings and spectacular views. This floor comprises the client meeting and fine-dining suite (with switchable glass walls, allowing the rooms to be obscured and confidential at the flick of a switch) and workstations for 500 employees.

The resulting dramatic and innovative design solution won the BCO National Award in 2014.

The design focuses on two oculus-shaped atria, and plays on maximizing light and views and on planning efficient spaces that radiate from the oculi.

Expedia

Various locations
Completed 2017–21

Scott Brownrigg was approached by Expedia in 2017 to inform a workplace strategy and future design that would keep pace with the company's meteoric global expansion. With the help of Design Strategy Unit, the interiors team re-engineered Expedia's engagement and design process to deliver improvements across all areas of performance of future office locations, including speed of delivery, capital cost, functionality and effectiveness in serving a specific population.

The practice used a bespoke work-style profiler questionnaire to identify the spatial needs of individuals, teams and the workforce as a whole. The results formed the basis of a live workplace standards guide, which enabled regional delivery teams to interpret the information and deliver highly bespoke yet functionally consistent workplaces around the world. This approach helped to ensure that new global workplaces were tailored to meet the functional, well-being and cultural needs of staff on a regional basis.

The first fit-out that Scott Brownrigg designed for Expedia was in Hamburg, Germany, and completed in 2017. Having acquired an up-and-coming global car-rental brand, Expedia was eager to create a new, vibrant home for the collaboration that would express a collective mission to enjoy the journey as well as the destination. In 2018 the practice designed two new Expedia offices in the Middle East, in Jordan and Dubai. Both blend Expedia culture with local influences and works from local artists and makers to create a sophisticated workplace that reflects its location.

In 2019 the practice helped Expedia to consolidate its group of brands in a 1950s building in Munich. Scott Brownrigg created an agile working environment with a variety of work settings, while maintaining a sophisticated interior, stylized around local and travel themes in the meeting rooms and open spaces. The industrial steel skeleton of the building remained intact, and incorporated new design elements influenced by the building's former use as a men's department store.

Following the growth in e-commerce, in 2021 Scott Brownrigg worked with Expedia to transform the Angel Building in London from multi-tenant to single occupancy, to become a new global hub. The 'campus'-style workplace is designed around flexibility, well-being and culture, and features a wide range of breakout and focus areas and informal meeting and touchdown spaces adjacent to primary circulation spaces to encourage interaction and collaboration between employees from diverse functions and disciplines. Building on a strong organizational culture designed around the concept of wanderlust and the reasons why people travel, the practice recognized that these interactions would, over time, result in a network of highly productive and trusting relationships.

The Expedia headquarters in London serves as a good example of how the traditional desk-based workplace has been replaced by a workpoint-focused solution.

Hard Rock Hotel London

Westminster, London
Completed 2019

The bar design drew inspiration from the Art Deco ceiling of the Lyons Corner House that stood on the site in the early 1900s. Other features, such as the fretboard wall displays (below), linked to the Hard Rock brand.

The practice transformed the Cumberland Hotel – situated in one of London's most prominent locations, on the corner of Oxford Street and Park Lane – into the four-star Hard Rock Hotel. The Cumberland had been a popular haunt for such music legends as Nina Simone, Stevie Wonder, Bob Dylan and Jimi Hendrix. The design focused primarily on the entrance and the ground-floor guest experience.

Reimagined in a contemporary way, the interior design drew inspiration both from the history of the mid-1700s building and from the iconic music and fashion fundamental to the Hard Rock brand. A curated collection of historical artefacts displayed throughout the hotel showcased the very best of British, American and international music. As well as celebrating the site's heritage, the forty-two-seat Lobby Bar featured an abstract installation of a master disc and a record player. Memorabilia was suspended from the walls among taut guitar strings, in a larger-than-life fretboard.

The project earned numerous industry accolades, including an International Hotel and Property Award in 2019 and a Mixology Award in 2020. In 2023 the hotel reverted to its previous name.

Hard Rock Hotel London
A curated collection of artefacts displayed throughout the hotel showcased the very best of British, American and international music.

ERIC CLAPTON, MORRISSEY AND THE EDGE
TAYLOR SWIFT
RELAX
DAVID BOWIE

Thomson Reuters

Canary Wharf, Tower
Hamlets, London
Completed 2020

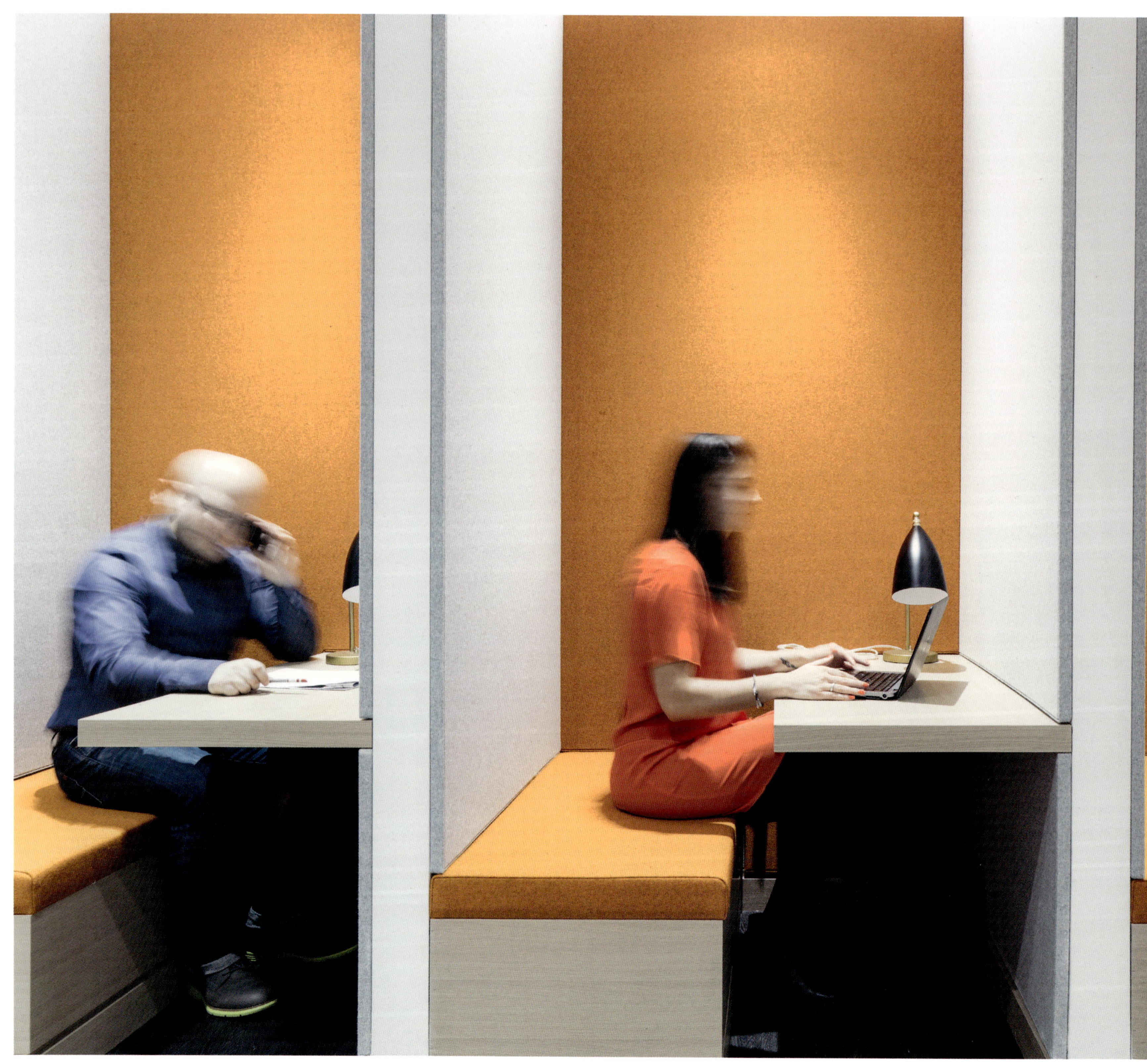

Faced with the need to consolidate some of its London sites and accommodate recent acquisitions and a growing team, the financial data provider Thomson Reuters briefed Scott Brownrigg to extend and fit out its existing office to create a 46,450-square-metre European Hub Headquarters at Canada Square.

Introducing the concept of agile and collaborative working, Thomson Reuters sought a solution that would provide employees with autonomy in how and where they work by creating a space that features a diverse range of work settings and promotes cooperation, productivity and flexibility. Fundamental to the design was the provision of a large hub on each floor that allows people to come together to help build closer collaborations. A vibrant colour palette reinforces the Thomson Reuters brand identity and highlights areas that foster interaction and flexibility. Graphics and manifestations are used to convey brand values and key messaging to employees.

Completed in 2017, the first phase of the development was used to benchmark new ways of working for the organization, and as a basis for establishing its global design standards, including future phases and associated projects designed by Scott Brownrigg in New York and Stamford, Connecticut. The final phase, which completed in 2020, culminated in the design of the newsroom for Thomson Reuters and associated TV studios and interview rooms.

Designs for Thomson Reuters promote interaction, and include a centrally located hub on each floor to maximize connectivity and collaboration.

Future Thinking: Interior Design

As people navigate the demands of modern life, spaces must adapt to provide versatility, comfort and functionality that cater to overlapping personal and professional needs. The future of interior design lies in its ability to anticipate and respond to these shifting dynamics.

Changes in working practices and advances in technology, combined with an increasing emphasis on employee well-being and user experience, are transforming the approach to workplace interior design. The ability to make informed, data-driven decisions is crucial to meeting the changing needs of organizations and their employees now and in the future, and spaces must be as diverse, adaptable and resilient as the organizations that they serve.

The future points towards a focus on creating adaptable and inclusive workplaces, designed to accommodate a wide range of work styles, with accessible features and sensory-friendly zones that enhance comfort and usability for all. Spaces dedicated to physical and mental activities, such as gyms, meditation rooms and relaxation zones, are becoming core features, helping employees to recharge and cultivate a balanced, healthy lifestyle.

The blending of hospitality with office environments and the activation of spaces such as reception to accommodate a variety of uses throughout the day and night create opportunity to foster interaction and community engagement and to generate additional income. The incorporation of areas within the workplace for the use of students or community groups contributes to a sense of inclusivity and connectivity, enhancing the building's role as a multifunctional, community-orientated environment.

Integration of the latest technology, such as AI and digital twins, will offer a powerful tool to enhance and personalize employee experience within the workplace, allowing for real-time adjustments that promote comfort, productivity and well-being.

As homes and hotels increasingly meet the same needs as workplaces, the lines between these environments will continue to blur, driving innovation and redefining what it means to design for human experience.

The global shift towards remote work and flexible schedules has created a demand for interiors that seamlessly integrate living, leisure and productivity. Spaces are no longer singularly defined.

Residential interiors are increasingly borrowing from hospitality design to create spaces that feel luxurious, curated and welcoming. Conversely, hotels are adapting to feel more residential, creating intimate, homelike environments that prioritize personalization and flexibility.

Technology is at the heart of the transformation, bridging the gap between personal and professional life. Smart home systems that control lighting, temperature and security are becoming standard in residential design, while hotels are leveraging similar technologies in order to enhance the guest experience. Seamless connectivity, high-speed internet and adaptable technology are fundamental features within successful flexible working environments.

Design is also responding to the human desire for connection. In residential spaces, communal areas encourage family interactions and socializing, while hotels are incorporating co-working spaces and communal lounges as a means of fostering collaboration and networking. The balance between private and shared spaces is critical to meeting evolving expectations.

Ultimately, the convergence of residential, hospitality and workplace design reflects a broader shift towards unified spaces that serve multiple roles. We are tasked with creating environments that are not only visually appealing but also versatile and adaptive; where every square metre serves a purpose while aligning with the user's lifestyle and values. An emphasis on minimizing waste and on designing environments that are both resource-efficient and future-ready can ensure that these spaces remain dynamic, functional and resilient in the long term.

Business + Science Parks

The evolution of business parks to science parks

Ed Hayden

Scott Brownrigg's transformation over the past few decades reflects a unique evolution within British architecture. From a reputation for designing business parks during the 1980s and '90s, the practice steadily turned towards a new frontier that saw these parks become increasingly occupied by organizations that focus on technology or pharmaceuticals, and, more recently, the rise of the science park, with a focus on life sciences. This evolution tells a broader story of the company's adaptability and commitment to advancing the quality of workplaces and to responding to the technological shifts that have transformed the landscape of business and science.

The practice became involved in designing business parks mainly in the 1980s, when demand for commercial spaces surged. At a time of rapid advancements in technology, business parks provided the perfect homes for burgeoning technology companies across the UK, and Scott Brownrigg was a pioneer in the design field.

Among the early projects were Watchmoor Park in Frimley, Waterside Park in Bracknell and Guildford Business Park, developed between 1986 and 1988. Embodying the practice's mission to create spaces that nurtured innovation, these developments attracted high-profile tenants such as Toshiba UK.

Demonstrating Scott Brownrigg's prowess for large-scale, complex developments, each park featured hallmark elements of the practice's design philosophy in this sector. Strategic accessibility was a key theme: site locations were chosen for visibility and ease of access, reflecting an early understanding of the need for connectivity in business. During the late 1980s and the 1990s, there was a growing acknowledgement of the importance of interiors designed for and adapted to a tenant's needs, as focus shifted towards achieving flexible layouts.

By the mid-1990s, the practice's business park expertise was well recognized throughout the industry and particularly across the Thames Valley.

In 1992 work began on the former Hatfield Aerodrome site for Arlington Securities, known later as Goodman. The practice was initially commissioned to develop the masterplan for a 323-hectare site. Its designs incorporated a new business district area with over 185,000 square metres of employment space, a campus for the University of Hertfordshire, and over 1000 new homes with access to a green central park, schools and a variety of community facilities. At the time, it was the largest masterplan in Europe to achieve planning consent. Scott Brownrigg delivered the first phase of the business district, which included plot 9600 for Arlington, comprising 4000 square metres of office and production area, and a 6500-square-metre facility for Royal Mail.

During this period, the practice's work in this sector reflected rapid technological advances, as Scott Brownrigg secured a series of projects for expanding technology companies seeking out-of-town locations. Designs for Computacenter at Hatfield included a 10,000-square-metre headquarters building and a 21,000-square-metre high-bay distribution warehouse with a multimillion-pound automatic picking-and-distribution system on the site. A yard accommodating eighteen loading docks, an associated marshalling area and car parking for some 1100 cars was also provided.

Heavily landscaped, with the inclusion of a storm-water lake, the sensitively designed complex belies its scale and impact. With the use of fast-track building methods, the development completed in just twenty months, in 1998.

The Hatfield campus for T-Mobile provides 50,500 square metres of workspace across a large, flexible campus that could operate as a single headquarters or a multi-tenant space. The major project delivered six buildings, each 7000 square metres, grouped formally around a central landscaped podium that sits above a 9000-square-metre basement car park. It completed in 2002, just two and half years after inception.

Owing to its fast-track nature, the project was procured through a design-and-build route, and at the time was one of the largest construction schemes in the UK to be managed through a project extranet. Two-thirds of the way through the construction period, T-Mobile instructed the

T-Mobile Headquarters, Hatfield Business Park
The T-Mobile headquarters building forms part of a wider 323-hectare masterplan at the former Hatfield Aerodrome site, for which Scott Brownrigg secured planning.

design of a dramatic three-storey glazed atrium to link the two central buildings and create a feature of the main entrance. Although it was a challenge to change the design at such at late stage, the adaptability of the phased buildings allowed for the inclusion of the new feature.

Oracle Corporation's headquarters at Thames Valley Park completed in 1996. Initially commissioned to reconfigure the 24-hectare masterplan, the practice went on to design the first phase, comprising 23,000 square metres of prime office space for Oracle. With designs that integrated the landscape and showcased structural innovations, the project earned accolades within the industry. The Oracle campus was one of the first in the Thames Valley to forsake the traditional design of business park buildings, which often saw schemes with pitched roofs, clad in brickwork and in many ways resembling a large house rather than an office building.

In the late 1990s and early 2000s, Bartley Wood Business Park in Hook, Hampshire, further enhanced Scott Brownrigg's reputation in this sector. The expansive, 75,500-square-metre development attracted such blue-chip tenants as BMW, NTL and Old Mutual. The Bartley Wood project marked a shift in workplace design, reflecting evolving expectations of office spaces. As quality of environment became increasingly important, designs focused on the provision of high-quality landscaping, the integration of water features and the retention of mature trees in order to create a more inviting work setting, one that supported employee well-being. Flexibility and responsiveness were also key drivers, facilitating future modifications to accommodate various building sizes and tenant needs.

Buildings such as Bartley Wood's 230/240 incorporated central atria so as to foster interaction – an architectural theme that would later be echoed in science parks, where collaborative spaces are integral.

The late 1990s brought Scott Brownrigg closer to the life sciences sector, setting the stage for a gradual shift as the practice was commissioned to design the 16-hectare masterplan and redevelopment of Howbery Park at Wallingford (pp. 104–105). Owned by the HR Wallingford Group, formerly the government's Hydraulics Research Station, the site comprised a range of commercial buildings, developed from the 1940s onwards, as well as a number of older listed buildings, most of which were deemed unsuitable to meet the needs of HR Wallingford.

Located within a sensitive landscape, the site was subject to restrictive planning policy aimed at restraining employment growth. Following the preparation of a masterplan and the submission of a planning application, South Oxfordshire District Council granted planning permission for new B1 office accommodation totalling some 13,000 square metres, in a scheme that involved demolition of some of the existing modelling halls. The first two buildings delivered from the masterplan were Red Kite House and Kestrel House, which collectively form the gateway into the park. Red Kite House (pp. 52–55) was an early example of sustainable office design for the practice. Rated BREEAM Excellent, it integrated wind turbines on its roof to support natural ventilation and was the first office in the UK to use turbines for this purpose. The building was opened by the chairman of the Environment Agency and the then MP for Henley, Boris Johnson, in 2005 and subsequently featured as part of that year's

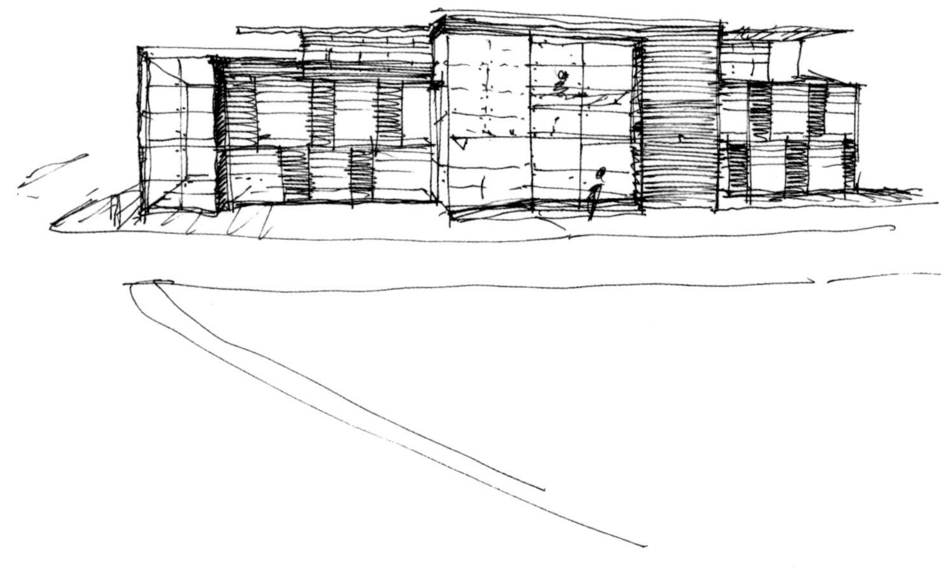

Foundation Park
Sketch of one of the refurbished buildings on the redeveloped Foundation Park masterplan.

BCO conference strand on sustainability, which was chaired by the practice CEO.

Much of Scott Brownrigg's success in the business park sector has resulted from the long-standing relationships it has had with leading developers. The practice was commissioned by PRUPIM in 1997 to masterplan Green Park in Reading (pp. 102–103), transforming 73 hectares of low-lying, partly contaminated agricultural land into what is now one of the UK's leading office parks, and providing both speculative and bespoke buildings. Design and delivery of phase one of the masterplan included the Symantec Campus, which comprised a total of 14,000 square metres of office accommodation across three buildings – 300, 350 and 400 Brook Drive – and completed in 2003.

Although pre-let to a major pharmaceutical company, 500 Brook Drive (completed 2009; pp. 56–57) provided flexible accommodation that would enable the building to be let to multiple occupiers in the future, if required. With both the base build and its fit-out recognized in a series of industry awards, 500 Brook Drive was a major success for the practice and set the benchmark for its future office designs.

Scott Brownrigg's involvement with Green Park continues today, on a subsequent phase for a further 320,000 square metres of land that include 140,000 square metres of business space. It has received planning consent for 23,700 square metres over six individual offices at 500–600 Longwater Avenue.

In 2004 the practice was commissioned by British Land, and subsequently Liberty Property Trust, to develop two new office buildings, Rhodium and Tungsten, on Blythe Valley Park, Solihull. The two buildings were designed to transform the architectural character of the existing business park, and resulted in a further commission for Scott Brownrigg to masterplan the second phase of the park. In 2007 consent was given for an additional 80,000 square metres of uniquely planned business space.

The second phase carefully considered the topography and existing landscaping, while creating a new public open space at the heart of the planned business park. When Liberty Property Trust took over the park in 2008, the practice was appointed to design two further office buildings of 3200 square metres and 2600 square metres. Scott Brownrigg subsequently took full ownership of the whole 200,000-square-metre business park masterplan, providing a plot-by-plot analysis and options for future tenants' requirements. In addition, it developed design codes for individual plots, enabling future buildings to be delivered in line with the overall vision and design standard for the park.

Building on its work at Green Park and Blythe Valley Park, Scott Brownrigg became involved with Frogmore Real Estate Partners Investment Managers on a redeveloped masterplan for Foundation Park in Maidenhead. The aim was to bring a new lease of life to the dated park with the refurbishment and extension (with new roof-level accommodation) of an initial two buildings, each of 2323 square metres, together with a new build of 4300 square metres, all completed in 2009. The site was sold to J.P. Morgan in 2015. Scott Brownrigg has continued its involvement in the development of the park with the design of three new buildings to provide increased capacity and amenity spaces.

Scott Brownrigg's journey into the life sciences began in Cambridge, a city renowned for its academic excellence and scientific innovation. The practice had already contributed to the region with its work on such projects as Cambridge Lakes (completed 2002) and Three Crowns House (completed 2011). Cambridge Science Park (pp. 106–109), which was established in 1970 by Trinity College, is one of the oldest and most prominent science parks in the world. It has been instrumental in the growth of the UK's technology and life sciences sectors. The park was founded with the vision of fostering collaboration between university researchers and businesses, offering companies proximity to the University of Cambridge's cutting-edge research facilities.

The practice's first project on the science park was the redevelopment of a building that dates back to 1973. Originally opened by the Duke of Edinburgh, this building was one of the first science facilities developed on the park. By 2008 it had become known as 101 Cambridge Science Park, and Scott Brownrigg was tasked with transforming the site during a time of financial turbulence. The global financial crisis of 2008–2009 was one of the most severe economic downturns since the Great Depression, and it had a significant impact on the UK economy. Despite these challenges, Building 101 completed and proved to be a remarkable success. It was fully let soon after completion and achieved the highest rental prices in the Cambridge market over the following decade.

This success drew the attention of TusPark (Tsinghua University Science Park), a large network of science and technology parks affiliated with Tsinghua University in Beijing. TusPark invested in the growing global prominence of Cambridge, helping to create an innovation ecosystem at Cambridge Science Park. In 2018 Scott Brownrigg was commissioned to develop state-of-the-art office and laboratory spaces for tech and life sciences companies, marking an important milestone in the practice's expanding role in the region.

The success of this project led to a collaboration with TusPark to create a Bio-Innovation Centre based on a pioneering 'Flex-Lab' concept. The Bio-Innovation Centre introduced modular lab spaces for start-ups, catering for the fast-paced life sciences sector by enabling tenants to scale up or down with minimal disruption. This innovative concept was the first of its kind on the

5 Foundation Park
Designed for J.P. Morgan Asset Management and completed in 2020, 5 Foundation Park introduces over 6130 square metres of new lettable area to the Maidenhead business park.

park. It created a dynamic environment for life sciences start-ups and contributed significantly to the park's transformation into a thriving hub for scientific innovation. The project led to further collaborations with TusPark – among them the development of 1–2 Cambridge Science Park – solidifying the practice's reputation as a leading architectural company in Cambridge's tech and life sciences sectors, while reinforcing its growing influence as a global design leader in science innovation spaces.

Consolidating its growing reputation, Scott Brownrigg's work in Cambridge continued when the practice was invited to participate in a design competition for the new headquarters of Arm Holdings, a global leader in semiconductor and software design (pp. 60–63).

Arm was founded in 1990 as a joint venture between Acorn Computers, Apple and VLSI Technology, and it played a critical role in the rise of mobile technology during the 1990s. The company had outgrown its home in Fulbourn Road and required a new facility for its expanding workforce.

At a memorable presentation, Mike Muller, Arm's co-founder and long-time chief technology officer, made a humorous yet pointed remark about the design for the new headquarters. He noted that 30 per cent of the facade featured curved elements and joked that '30 per cent of the design is wrong.' To which the practice responded, 'That means 70 per cent is right!' This light-hearted exchange marked the beginning of a successful working relationship as Scott Brownrigg set about designing a headquarters that would meet the company's unique needs.

A key element of the design was a request that the CEO should be able to address all staff members in one space, with every employee having a clear line of sight. This requirement became the guiding principle for what would become a 'ground scraper', with a single, expansive room designed to accommodate the entire Arm team. At the heart of the design is an internal 'town square', a large central space where all walkways, balconies and floors converge, creating a visually connected and cohesive environment that promotes collaboration and showcases the firm's capacity for innovative problem-solving. That this ambitious concept came to life is a testament to the success of the project and the strong sense of community it fosters within the Arm family.

Completion of Arm's headquarters led to further success stories in Cambridge, among them The Optic for British Land, and Cambridge International Technology Park (pp. 114–15), which includes 48,300 square metres of laboratory and office space catering for biotechnology and life sciences, while also accommodating traditional office needs. These developments extended the footprint of the Fulbourn Road area, supporting the continued growth of the 'Silicon Fen' tech cluster around Arm and further enhancing Cambridge's global reputation as a centre for technology and life sciences innovation.

Recent projects at Cambridge Biomedical Campus – 1, 2 and 3 Discovery Drive – provide life sciences laboratories.

In recent years, Scott Brownrigg's science park expertise has expanded to Oxford, where Eastpoint Business Park has been redeveloped into a life sciences campus. Integrating 20,000 square metres of laboratory and office space, Eastpoint reflects the practice's approach to merging functional and communal spaces, which are essential for both research and well-being.

The practice has also been actively involved in the development of new facilities at The Oxford Science Park (pp. 110–13), which is strategically located within one of the UK's leading science and technology hubs. Having won the design competition, Scott Brownrigg designed three new buildings on the park, totalling over 40,000 square metres, to serve as headquarters for various science and technology companies.

Majority-owned by Magdalen College, The Oxford Science Park is designed to foster innovation, discovery and entrepreneurship. The new buildings are constructed on plots 23–26 and are part of a broader ambition to expand the park's offerings, addressing a significant demand for high-quality laboratory and office space in the Oxford area. The development includes well-designed environments that promote sustainability and biodiversity, with pedestrian-friendly layouts that can accommodate cafes and co-working spaces at ground level.

These projects aim to support scientific innovation while also fostering community engagement and STEM outreach, continuing Scott Brownrigg's holistic development approach – namely, to balance laboratory and office needs, catering for a diverse tenant base and enhancing productivity; to reflect a long-standing commitment to sustainable, health-conscious design, an essential element for the life sciences sector; and to support initiatives that promote Science Technology Engineering and Mathematics (STEM) learning and engagement with the local community, reflecting a belief in development that benefits society as a whole.

1 Discovery Drive, Cambridge Biomedical Campus
1 Discovery Drive is a speculatively designed five-storey multi-occupancy building at Cambridge Biomedical Campus that combines flexible laboratory and office uses to suit a range of end users.

Green Park

Reading, Berkshire
1997 onwards

The development of Green Park in Reading transformed 73 hectares of low-lying, partly contaminated agricultural land into what is now one of the UK's leading office parks. Situated at Junction 11 of the M4, the park comprised both speculative development and bespoke building design while offering a coherent approach to office accommodation. The masterplan would enable a better way of working: imaginative landscaping and views over Longwater Lake, coupled with enhanced transportation links, set the scene for exemplary workplace provision across a variety of unit sizes.

The site originally had planning permission for 225,000 square metres of predominantly business-orientated space divided among fourteen plots, each with its own access to the park's road network. The first phase saw completion of the Symantec Campus in 2003. Designed by Scott Brownrigg, the campus provided 14,000 square metres of office accommodation across three buildings: 300, 350 and 400 Brook Drive. The vision was for a 'collegiate' setting around a central piazza for one occupier, while creating a series of buildings that could equally be viewed as separate investment packages – a concept that would carry through to future development.

Completed in 2009, 450 Brook Drive combines over 3000 square metres of flexible office space across three storeys with views over Longwater Lake, creating the perfect balance between a functional and a tranquil corporate headquarters. Finally, 500 Brook Drive (completed 2009; pp. 56–57) provides 13,000 square metres of workspace over five storeys. On a prominent corner plot at Green Park visible from the M4, the design creates a strong visual approach along South Oak Way towards Brook Drive. The sustainable credentials of the project became integral to the design. Both the developer and the tenant drove the energy efficiency of the building and its future reduction in carbon consumption, resulting in a BREEAM Excellent rating for the business park.

The park established a green travel plan that incorporates a co-owned fleet of low-emission buses – some of the first in the UK designed to meet the stringent Euro 4 emissions standard – and sets out designated cycle routes across the site. Green Park is also home to a large solo wind turbine that produces 2 MW of electricity and serves over 1000 homes in the local area.

Since its development, the business park has established itself as a hub for technology-based companies, including world leaders in the fields of software and the internet.

A long-standing relationship with PRUPIM and now Mapletree has enabled the practice to masterplan, design and deliver buildings at Green Park from the late 1990s to the present day. The first project was the Symantec Campus (below). Opposite: Masterplan of Green Park with Scott Brownrigg buildings highlighted orange.

Howbery Business Park

Wallingford,
Oxfordshire
Completed 2009

Howbery is where history meets innovation in support of a vision for a characterful, sustainable business park in Oxfordshire. The masterplan for the redevelopment of Howbery Park at Wallingford was designed to attract a diverse range of businesses to a site with high-quality amenities set in a stunning natural setting providing opportunities to develop and thrive.

A detailed assessment of the 16-hectare site and existing buildings – some of which were listed and many others outdated and unsuitable to meet the operational requirements of HR Wallingford – enabled the practice to maximize development potential and maintain a new approach to business park planning that encouraged scientific interaction with nature.

The first two buildings to be delivered from the masterplan were Red Kite House (pp. 52–55), which was designed as the headquarters for the Environment Agency, and Kestrel House. Both curved in plan, they collectively form an impactful gateway into the park. On the completion of Kestrel House in 2009, Howbery Park was one of few business parks in the UK to house two buildings with a BREEAM Excellent rating.

Supporting the park's sustainable agenda, Red Kite House and Kestrel House have acted as catalysts for future development on-site. Opposite: Site plan of Howbery Business Park with Red Kite House and Kestrel House highlighted orange.

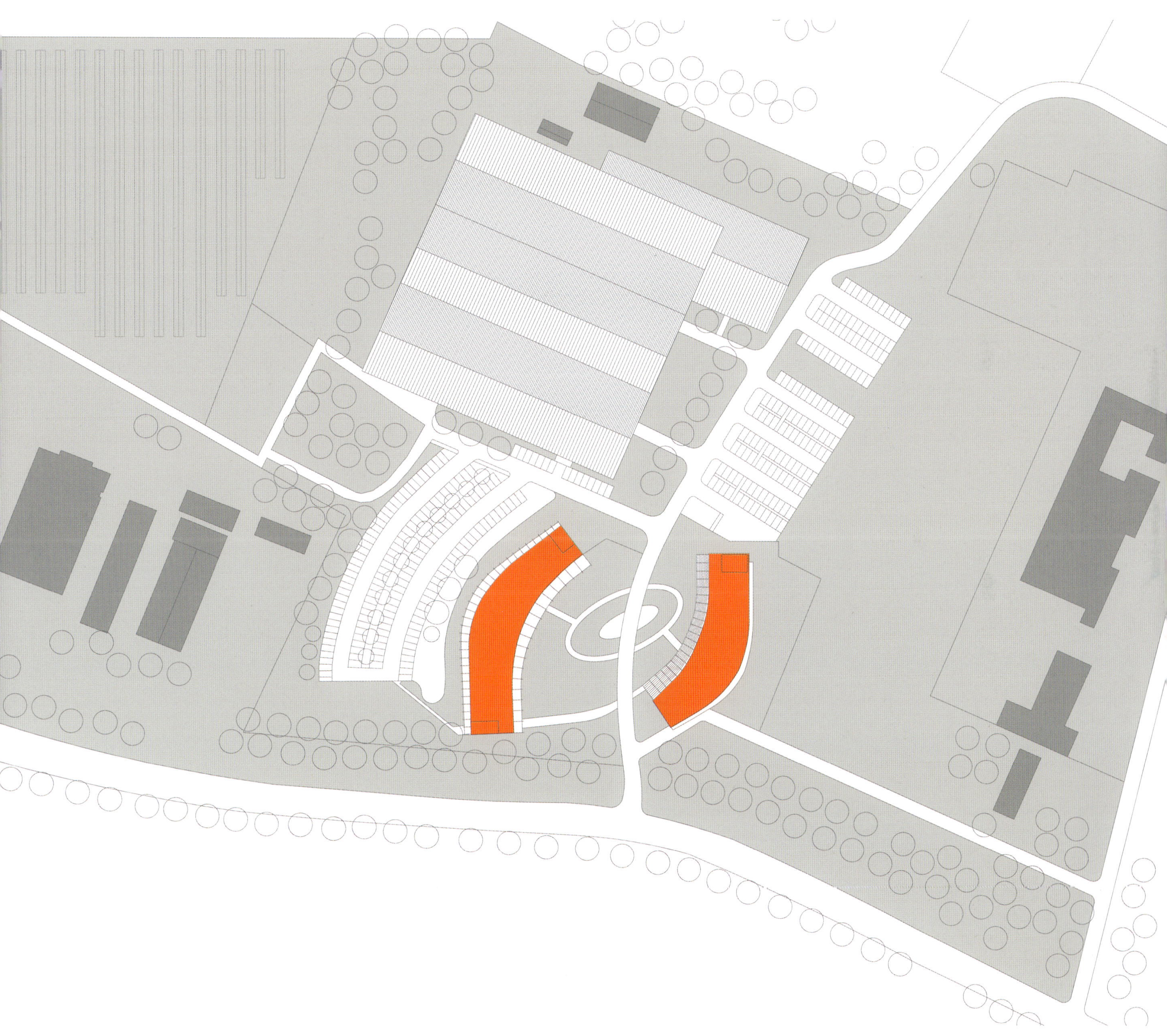

Cambridge Science Park

Cambridge
Completed 2021

Scott Brownrigg has been instrumental in shaping Cambridge Science Park into a global hub for science, innovation and sustainability, and has elevated its architectural identity, blending functionality with elegance to meet the evolving needs of its cutting-edge tenants.

The Bio-Innovation Centre encompasses plots 22, 25 and 26. With state-of-the-art laboratories and versatile workspaces that support both established companies and emerging innovators, this £65 million development reflects the park's ethos of fostering world-class research and development.

The three-storey Frontier Developments building, designed for plot 26, integrates seamlessly into its surroundings, with a landscaped podium and discreet parking solutions that emphasize sustainability. Achieving a BREEAM Excellent rating, it exemplifies the park's commitment to creating environments that inspire productivity while prioritizing environmental stewardship. Projects such as plots 1–21 and the Bio-Innovation Centre demonstrate a shared design language of refined simplicity, with interiors designed for adaptability, and modular labs and office spaces catering to tenants' shifting needs, ensuring long-term relevance and appeal.

Beyond individual buildings, Scott Brownrigg's masterplanning contributions have transformed the park into a harmonious and people-centric environment, not only enhancing its architectural landscape but also driving its vision of innovation and community. By prioritizing flexibility, sustainability and user-centric design, the firm has helped to position the park as a model for science-driven developments worldwide.

Each new building is carefully designed to reinforce Cambridge Science Park's status as a world-leading technology and science centre and to help attract the best organizations and talent. Opposite: Masterplan of Cambridge Science Park with Scott Brownrigg buildings highlighted orange.

Overleaf: Plots 1–21 create a new gateway to Cambridge Science Park, with a sweeping colonnade that signposts the entrance and invites occupants and visitors in.

The Oxford Science Park

Oxford
Concept designed 2022

Three new buildings at The Oxford Science Park (TOSP) will provide over 40,000 square metres of office and laboratory space, offering a flexible environment for established science and technology companies and newcomers alike. The development includes plots 23–26, which will not only support the growth of existing tenants but also enable the park to welcome new businesses into its thriving community. This expansion reinforces Oxford's reputation as a global leader in scientific discovery and innovation.

Designed with sustainability and well-being at their core, the buildings emphasize high-quality, flexible spaces that are adaptable to changing needs. The four-storey structures will feature active frontages, including cafes and co-working areas on the ground floor, creating vibrant, welcoming spaces for collaboration. A series of external working areas and amenities will connect the buildings, providing a variety of outdoor spaces where users can interact and work.

The landscape design prioritizes biodiversity, incorporating native plant species that enhance the park's ecological value. Brown roofs are included on each building where possible, contributing to the park's environmental sustainability. Thoughtful design ensures that each building maximizes natural light, reducing reliance on artificial lighting and cooling. The use of passive-design principles promotes energy efficiency, while the buildings' flexibility allows them to be easily reconfigured or reused in the future.

This development is a key step in ensuring that TOSP continues to support the growth of the Oxford–Cambridge Arc and solidifies its position as a leading centre for research, development and innovation.

The development of plots 23–26 enables new companies to join The Oxford Science Park's unique community.

Overleaf: The three new buildings are part of ambitious long-term development plans to help meet demand through the creation of exemplary additional office and laboratory space.

Peterhouse Technology Park and Cambridge International Technology Park

Cambridge
Completed 2024;
concept designed 2020

In 2019 the practice played a pivotal role in the expansion of Peterhouse Technology Park on the outskirts of Cambridge, designing a new headquarters for the globally renowned technology company Arm (pp. 60–63). This project not only underscored the park's prominence in the tech landscape but also acted as a catalyst for future growth, cementing the site as a hub of innovation.

Scott Brownrigg went on to spearhead the design of the next phase of development, The Optic, an 8800-square-metre facility offering flexible office and lab-enabled workspaces. Targeted at science and technology companies, this project exemplifies the firm's commitment to creating versatile environments tailored to the needs of Cambridge's dynamic market.

Adjacent to Peterhouse Technology Park, Cambridge International Technology Park represents the next frontier in life sciences and technology spaces. Envisioned as a 48,300-square-metre facility, it will cater for life sciences, biotechnology and office occupiers. Speculative designs allow for multi- or single-tenant use, emphasizing adaptability for a wide array of businesses.

Together, these two technology parks are set to form a southern Cambridge science hub of international significance. By addressing the critical demand for high-quality laboratory and office spaces, Scott Brownrigg's designs support the region's reputation as a world-leading centre for research and development, and demonstrate how innovative architectural design can drive economic and scientific growth.

Buildings on Cambridge International Technology Park feature covered outdoor collaborative workspaces within a series of landscaped terraces, providing tenants with ultimate flexibility in where they work. Below: Masterplan of Peterhouse Technology Park and Cambridge International Technology Park with Scott Brownrigg buildings highlighted orange.

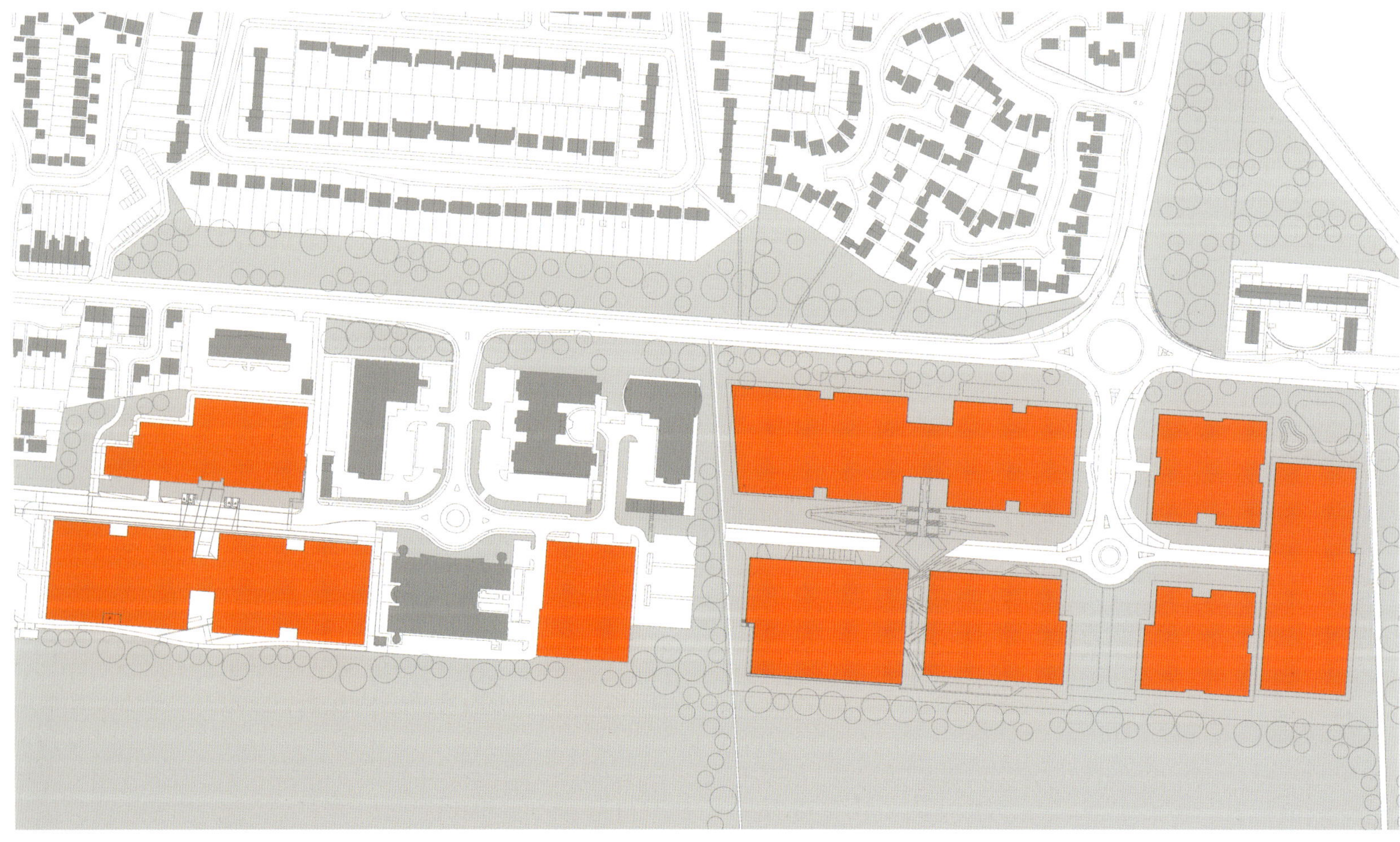

Future Thinking: Business + Science Parks

Science and business parks of the future are about creating people-centric environments that encourage innovation, collaboration and community engagement; that contribute to quality of place while creating opportunities for education and economic growth.

The global demand for new and reimagined business and life sciences space continues to grow as building owners look to secure longer-term leases, occupiers seek to attract and retain staff, and the industry moves towards net zero. Campuses of the future therefore need to cater for a diverse tenant base, facilitate flexibility in use, and reflect a commitment to sustainable, health-conscious design – an essential element for the life sciences sector and an increasing focus for business-space occupiers.

By combining cutting-edge technology and innovative materials and construction techniques, and through a commitment to ecological harmony, the industry's approach to sustainable building practices can be redefined. Scott Brownrigg has been exploring ways in which adopting a 'long life, loose fit' design approach and opting for a hybrid structure can reduce embodied carbon associated with new-build laboratory buildings, while simultaneously ensuring that they are flexible enough to meet a range of end-user needs in the future.

The practice has also been exploring the viability of changing other building typologies for life sciences, with ongoing projects that transform redundant retail spaces on the high street and outdated office buildings into laboratories. This creates valuable opportunities not only to retain and revitalize existing building stock, but also to support initiatives that promote and increase access to STEM learning and encourage greater engagement with the local community, breaking down barriers and putting science on show.

As advances in technology provide more flexibility in the choice of where people can work, the spaces between buildings on business and science parks or adjacent to inner-city retrofits harbour potential to become just as important as the building itself. This is especially the case when they are treated as an extension of the building and used to create a variety of additional spaces where people can work, rest and socialize in a different setting. Placing more emphasis on landscaped spaces enables us to increase biodiversity net gain and deal with surface water, thereby creating opportunities to connect with nature and foster a greater sense of community.

Scott Brownrigg's evolution from business parks to science hubs highlights its adaptability, innovation and deepening understanding of the science sector's unique needs. Its early commitment to creating adaptable, high-quality and sustainable workspaces laid the groundwork for its eventual foray into life sciences. Now, as life sciences grow rapidly, the business stands poised to shape the future of scientific research through thoughtful, collaborative design. Scott Brownrigg's influence in Cambridge, Oxford and beyond marks it as a leader not just in architecture but also in the cultivation of environments that enable breakthrough discoveries.

Rail

Alarm

Creating infrastructure for seamless travel

Andrew Postings

The architect's role in transport goes beyond forming building envelopes. It encompasses the creation of spaces for transition and transactions and for linking activities, and it extends into planning of the urban realm. It involves collaborating with not only the building design disciplines but also alignment and geotechnical engineers, transport planners and operators.

Scott Brownrigg has undertaken architectural design and station-planning roles in many cities worldwide, delivering high-quality rail and metro transport projects. The practice's transport and infrastructure work has ranged from the architectural concepts for entire systems to detailed design, repair and refurbishment programmes.

In the late 1980s and early 1990s, the practice, working alongside Maunsell, was extensively involved in the design of ten new Docklands Light Railway (DLR) stations on the Beckton extension, using a standard system of components to form a kit of parts. The extension added 8 kilometres of double track and provided a vital link to new facilities along the Royal Docks, including ExCeL London and the University of East London Docklands Campus. Designed to a new 'house style', the kit made possible a range of station configurations above and below ground level. Clear routes and signage are a key component of such stations where passengers transit between trains, and between train and bus. The knowledge and expertise created by this project, combined with previous DLR work, strengthened the practice's offering to the market.

The second large DLR project was the £3 million depot building at Beckton. Completed and operational in early 1993, the depot was used to service and maintain the trains plying the DLR. The project was an early example of the importance of having a multidisciplinary team on complex rail projects. Work by the practice on the DLR has continued to the current day.

The sector was bolstered in 2004 when Design Research Unit (DRU) joined Scott Brownrigg and was integrated in the transport team. It is no exaggeration to say that DRU has influenced the way generations of people interact with the urban environment, having been responsible for some of the most important design produced in post-war Britain, including wayfinding graphics for the London Transport Executive, Westminster street signs and interiors for the P&O Orient Line's SS *Oriana*, to name just a few projects.

In 1963 DRU started to devise a new image for the British Rail transportation system. The British Rail corporate identity programme was the largest and most complex undertaken in the UK at the time. The company name was shortened from British Railways to British Rail, and Gerry Barney's two-way arrow became its new emblem. This logo set a standard for the period and became a prototype for similar organizations worldwide.

In 1965 DRU devised British Rail's *Corporate Identity Manual*, which gave detailed instructions for applying the logo and identity across all aspects of the business, from train liveries and station signage to staff uniforms and crockery. The identity was launched with the exhibition *The New Face of British Railways* at the Design Centre. The Rail Alphabet typeface was spaced on 'tiles' to ensure a consistent compact arrangement, while station signs used a stacked 'plank system' concept, which allowed for mass manufacture, cost effectiveness and ease of maintenance across the whole network. The new corporate identity extended beyond the appearance of 2000 stations; 4000 locomotives, 23,000 passenger carriages and forty-five Sealink ferries were also repainted on its implementation.

Despite British Rail's services now being franchised to private-sector operators, the original signage is still present in many stations, and the British Rail symbol can still be seen on every station facade and every ticket.

In 1964 DRU co-founder Misha Black, who was a professor of industrial design at the Royal College of Art, undertook a twelve-year consultancy at the London Transport Executive. He became responsible for all aspects of design for the Victoria line. Around 22 kilometres long and serving sixteen stations, it was the first deep-level Underground line to be built across central London for over fifty years. On its opening in 1968, it was considered the most advanced underground railway in the world, with the introduction of computer-controlled trains improving energy, time and cost efficiencies all around.

A frieze at the top of each platform wall, repeating the name of the station, allowed for easy recognition by passengers during busy

British Rail
Design Research Unit's globally recognized corporate identity and logo developed for British Rail in 1965 by Gerry Barney.

periods. Ceramic tile murals referring to the station name or its locality were commissioned for the platforms. The tiled designs in each seat recess provided colour and decoration, and gave each stop its own visual identity. Murals for Tottenham Hale, Highbury and Islington, and Victoria were designed by Edward Bawden, and the Stockwell mural by Abram Games. Train carriages were redesigned, and the corporate identity for London Transport introduced a plain-colour version of the roundel for use on Underground trains and buses. Misha Black received a knighthood in 1972.

Simultaneously, DRU was expanding its rail work overseas. In 1970 it commenced work on Hong Kong's first mass transit railway system, known as the Modified Initial System (MIS). The team formed the architectural and station-planning component of a UK engineering consortium that included Freeman Fox. A DRU Hong Kong office was established to service this project and the subsequent Kwun Tong line project. Today the Hong Kong Mass Transit Railway (MTR) handles over 2.4 million passengers a day and is among the busiest urban rail systems in the world.

The DRU Hong Kong office carried out a range of rail work, from early concept and feasibility work through to detail design and completion. Some of the work was at a strategic level, advising the MTR Corporation on developing smaller, more efficient station space.

In 1995 DRU was shortlisted with Dennis Lau & Ng Chun Man to provide architectural services on future extensions. Maunsell subsequently led

Copenhagen Metro
The Copenhagen Metro features striking glass pyramids on the roofs of its underground stations to allow natural light to illuminate the platforms below.

the group, which included DRU and secured the Tseung Kwan O and Quarry Bay extensions. Work on the Mass Transit Railway would last until 2003.

During this time, DRU carried out numerous additional rail-based projects in Hong Kong, including: a study on the total refurbishment of all thirty-eight stations of the operating railway; the study of a new line utilizing land available through the relocation of Kai Tak Airport (East Kowloon line); architectural planning and space standards of a new generation of typical stations on the Ma On Shan line; Wanchai station improvements; Kowloon Tong station congestion relief; East Tsim Sha Tsui interface study; North Point Congestion Relief Works; and Quarry Bay Congestion Relief Works.

The delivery of nine stations for Bangkok's Mass Rapid Transit (MRT) project was also led from the DRU Hong Kong office. The initial system of the Bangkok MRT comprised a single nineteen-station line from Hua Lamphong in the south to Bang Sue in the north. It was planned with interchange links to the later Orange line and the Bangkok Elevated Transit System. The design details were developed with the engineering team, led by Arup.

As architect to a construction joint venture, DRU was responsible for station planning and the design of nine stations on the northern section of the line. Station entrances were an important element to integrate into the Thai environment, while the cut-and-cover construction, generally within existing road corridors, formed the enclosure for developing station interiors. Underground spaces were planned with potential links to adjacent retail and development areas.

The DRU Hong Kong office included landscaping and urban design disciplines, enabling the portfolio of work to be expanded into non-rail areas in both Hong Kong and the wider region, including China.

Just prior to joining Scott Brownrigg, DRU completed work on six stations as part of the £1.3 billion Copenhagen Metro for AECOM. Procuring the project through a design-and-build contract, DRU provided full architectural services for station planning and the underground section of the works. The design work was developed on a site-by-site basis to suit the townscape and technical requirements.

In the UK, DRU applied its transit system expertise to the 14-kilometre Nottingham Express Transit (NET). Working for Carillion under a design-and-build contract, DRU provided architecture, landscaping and sign design services. The line consisted of twenty-three tram stops – six of which included extensive park-and-ride facilities – and ran through the historic city centre, terminating at Nottingham's mainline station. The tram-stop design adopted a kit of parts used in a variety of combinations to suit various site conditions at both on- and off-street stops. A tram depot and various system-related buildings also formed part of the brief. With its links to the motorway network, bus and other rail systems, NET has provided a truly integrated transport system benefiting the city's residents, visitors and businesses since its completion in 2004.

In 2018 Scott Brownrigg acquired the rail specialists Acanthus Architects LW to add team numbers and skills and maintain its strength in the rail sector. Acanthus brought not only its heritage projects but also new ones, such as Hounslow East station, Meridian Water Network Rail station in the London Borough of Enfield, Tottenham Court Road station, Crossrail Paddington Bakerloo Line Link, the Metropolitan Line Extension and Bath Spa station listed-building works as part of the Great Western Electrification Project.

Scott Brownrigg's multisector and multidisciplinary nature has given the rail sector the advantage of having in-house access to specialists, including urban designers, interior designers, technical advisers, and business space, retail and residential experts. This expertise often reduces the need to appoint

Meridian Water Station
Allowing step-free access and a 24-hour public right of way over an operational railway, Meridian Water station in Enfield has unlocked one of London's largest brownfield regeneration sites.

other consultants and enables the team to comprehensively manage and execute schemes that, as part of the station coordination and consultation process, take full advantage of all established stakeholder contacts.

A high level of knowledge of, and expertise in, the aspects of transportation design includes an understanding of the following: passenger-handling and circulation criteria; safety, particularly in respect of operation and fire; the requirements and drivers of inclusive and equitable design; facilities for intermodal interchange; wayfinding and navigation; security, control and operation; and maintenance requirements of the station. An understanding of the relationship between the railway and other commercial activities within the station, such as retail, enhances the offer.

The early 2000s saw Scott Brownrigg commissioned as the designers for Tube Lines, the company responsible for the Jubilee, Northern and Piccadilly lines under the public–private partnership (PPP) government initiative on the London Underground. The practice formed a designer joint venture to provide the full extent of professional services necessary to carry out the planned programme of modernizations and enhancements required under the PPP contract. The firm worked in partnership with Tube Lines and the contractor Morgan Est to develop, scope and agree a consistent design approach to the largest collection of important modernist buildings in the UK – the Piccadilly line stations of Charles Holden. Eighteen stations were delivered in the programme of works over a five-year period. This experience was key to securing much of the practice's future Underground work.

Addressing the needs of people with mobility restrictions, visual or aural impairment, or neurodivergent or neurodegenerative conditions, and those of both young and ageing populations, Scott Brownrigg has been the architect for numerous step-free-access projects over the years. Towards the end of the noughties, the practice was the architect for the Tube Lines New Works Step-Free Access Programme, which sought to increase access to the Underground network among a wider range of the population. Working within a multidisciplinary design team, the firm developed eight schemes through to conceptual design statement stage, including schemes involving listed buildings and below- and above-ground stations. This package of works enabled the practice to bring volume benefits, among them a consistent developed approach, confidence of client and assurance entities delivered to programme. It also brought Scott Brownrigg to the forefront of inclusive design.

The practice was appointed to facilitate step-free access to Green Park station in time for the 2012 Olympic Games through the addition of new lifts and ramped access from the park into the ticket hall. The new entrance facing Piccadilly contributes a civic element to a previously underused station entrance. Both the facade of a station and its entrance can have a significant impact on the public realm.

The Green Park design provides a prominent entrance with an active frontage composed of high-quality materials and green walls that act as a beacon in the landscape and environment of the Royal Park. Incorporated into the Portland stone cladding of the street-level shelter is an artwork titled *Sea Strata* by the Royal Academician John Maine. The Diana Fountain was relocated from its original site in the middle of the park to form the centrepiece of the new entrance.

Other London Underground work includes Hounslow East station, a project won in competition against three other London Underground framework architects. The station incorporates the first constant-radius timber lamella roof to have been constructed since the 1930s. In line with what was a relatively recent Transport for London initiative at the time, step-free access was achieved through the provision of a new street-level ticket hall and a lift to each platform. The scheme won the HSBC Station Excellence of the Year Award in 2006.

In 2005 the practice was appointed for the initial stages of the Victoria Underground station upgrade, part of Transport for London's five-year, £10 billion investment programme. Concept designs aimed to reduce severe congestion during peak travel times, which resulted in the regular enforcement of station-control measures. Works increased the size of the station by 50 per cent, with a new ticket hall, lifts and escalators to ease congestion and provide step-free access from street level to the Victoria, Circle and District lines.

In 2018 Scott Brownrigg delivered the remodelled Bond Street station to accommodate additional demand forecast for the Elizabeth line. The scheme provided a new entrance, additional escalators, interchange to Bond Street Elizabeth line station, and improvements to interchange and step-free access between lines.

The scheme at Tottenham Court Road station (pp. 134–35) provided a station modernization and congestion relief, with a significantly enlarged ticket hall below the streets, new entrances (including creating public realm at the front of Centre Point), step-free access to platforms and additional escalator inclines and back-of-house areas. The practice was intrinsically involved in the incorporation of the feature artwork – Daniel Buren's *Diamonds and Circles*, the French artist's first permanent public commission in the UK.

As part of AECOM's multidisciplinary team, Scott Brownrigg designed the new passenger link between the Paddington Elizabeth line station and the Bakerloo line Underground station. The deep-tunnel scheme (completed 2018), accessed from platform level at both stations, minimized damage to the Brunel-designed, Grade I-listed mainline station above, which was of significant concern to the overall Crossrail project team. Working in an extremely constrained environment, Scott Brownrigg developed designs using Bentley 3D software, which helped to gain stakeholder support. In demonstrating the feasibility of the scheme, the practice achieved a Transport and Works Act order without a lengthy public inquiry.

The scheme was extensively tested against client expectations for pedestrian flow, damage mitigation, constructability and fire strategy. It was threaded 17 metres below the Network Rail concourse level, avoiding nineteenth- and twentieth-century shafts, including conveyor inclines and deep-level tunnels. Consideration was also given to the impact on the now-disused Mail Rail station beneath the former Royal Mail sorting office.

Step-free access and heritage conservation skills were demonstrated in 2019 at Mill Hill East and Cockfosters stations, where knowledge of the London Underground environment and its systems and processes enabled the practice to develop a scalable and deliverable step-free-access solution, adaptable to all surface London Underground stations. Proposals were developed in conjunction with the London Underground Design Governance Board and local authority conservation officers.

Approval was given to use a masonry cladding system both to reduce critical overall dimensions within dimensionally constrained locations and to deliver significant reductions to the construction programme (led by the contractor Morgan Sindall). The small-scale modularity of the cladding system allowed for site adaptation while improving and complementing adjacent Grade II-listed fabric. The designs required extensive coordination with conservation officers and the integrated design team, including structural, mechanical, electrical, communications and lift engineers. As a result of these schemes, Scott Brownrigg is developing further installations to provide a lasting legacy for the travelling public.

The most recently completed work on the London Underground, at the Paddington Bakerloo line station (pp. 136–37), provides capacity enhancements to the existing station, including an expanded ticket hall and step-free access to the platforms. The station has been accepted into use and is now serving the travelling public. The practice worked in conjunction with the engineers WSP and Renzo Piano Building Workshop, architect of the adjacent Paddington Square development. The station is a third-party-funded project by the developer Sellar Properties.

Opportunities for the practice continue in the rail sector across global locations, most recently in Singapore: ongoing work on Tavistock station is the first rail project for Scott Brownrigg in the city state. The SGD 407 million new station forms part of the first phase of the Land Transport Authority's Cross Island Line, which will benefit more than 100,000 households and is set to be the longest fully underground line in Singapore's Mass Rapid Transit (MRT) system.

Tavistock station is designed to achieve Green Mark Platinum certification and will be constructed beneath Ang Mo Kio Avenue 3. Once complete, it will provide fast, efficient and sustainable transport for residents and workers in the neighbourhood. The scheme, which has four separate entrances, features a 'Park Connected' concept, which links the surface buildings, parks and greenery with the below-ground elements and ties the station into the local context. Informing the choice of materials, colours and textures, the concept connects three different communities and allows for future interchange and development.

Successful involvement in such long-term major projects for the public sector highlights a consistent record of delivery, design excellence, value for money and sustainability, while demonstrating constant imagination and creative flair. This level of experience, coupled with the application of technical skills and a teamwork sensibility, provides an exceptional level of design focus on all projects.

Docklands Light Railway

London
Completed 2010

Work on London's Docklands Light Railway (DLR) was extensive and included Bank station, West India Quay, Blackwall station, City Airport, the control centre at Poplar and a range of passenger-enhancement studies that completed in 2009. These involved the design and detailing of station-lengthening works at five stations on the DLR Beckton line, among them works at Custom House and Prince Regent to support use of the ExCeL facilities for the 2012 Olympic Games.

Completed in 2010 as part of the £1 billion DLR upgrade for AECOM, South Quay station was hailed by the infrastructure firm as 'an extraordinary feat of engineering'. The project effectively moved a whole station without any disruption to passengers. Use of clever engineering techniques ensured that the replacement station could be constructed without having to close the line or the old station.

Work on the DLR also involved detailed design and delivery. The landmark Langdon Park station was opened by the Mayor of London in December 2007 and won the British Construction Industry Regeneration Award in October 2008.

South Quay Station
South Quay DLR station (above) stretches across Millwall Inner Dock, with a full-length canopy providing weather protection for waiting passengers and two ground-level concourses.

Langdon Park Station
In recognition of the significant benefits it would bring to the local community, Langdon Park station (above and overleaf) was funded by the government's Community Infrastructure Fund and Leaside Regeneration.

Langdon Park
Information

LANGDON PARK
Tickets
Information
Route finder
Trains for Lewisham
Platform 2

Piccadilly Line

London
Completed 2010

In the early 2000s Scott Brownrigg was commissioned to carry out the designs for the public–private partnership station modernization and enhancement programme of works on the Piccadilly line in London. The programme involved the modernization and refurbishment across the Piccadilly line of Underground stations dating from the 1920s and early 1930s, including Sudbury Town, Knightsbridge and Arnos Grove.

Individual stations were evaluated, a process that involved assessing characteristics, integrity and viability while also factoring in scope requirement, listed status and features of significant historic importance. A line-wide exercise was carried out in conjunction with English Heritage to ensure that there was consistency in approach and detail across all stations in the programme. The awarded Piccadilly line stations are considered important examples of early modernist buildings, designed specifically in an identifiable British style.

The practice was later appointed to facilitate step-free access to Green Park station in time for the 2012 Olympic Games. The upgrade includes a new canopy over the previously underused entrance on the south side of Piccadilly, an enlarged staircase leading from the ticket hall to street level, and a new ramped entrance – centred around the relocated Diana Fountain – with views of the Royal Park. Embedded in the Portland stone cladding of the station canopy is a fossil-inspired artwork by John Maine RA titled *Sea Strata*.

Green Park Station
A new step-free entrance to Green Park station has transformed the public realm and created a new beacon in the landscape.

Tottenham Court Road Station

Westminster, London
Completed 2017

Completed in 2017 as part of a wider programme of works at Tottenham Court Road, a new Oxford Street corner entrance provides congestion relief at this busy interchange station. To deal with an ever-increasing demand, Scott Brownrigg delivered well-planned spaces, with efficient engineering that is both functional and delightful.

The scheme comprises the modernization of Central line interchange tunnels and platforms, including new stairs, a new operations building and the introduction of step-free access from street to platforms, with new lifts dropping down over 25 metres to platform level.

Application of the principles of London Underground's design language created a sense of order, comfort and security that is consistent with the network and its heritage. The practice was intrinsically involved in the incorporation of the feature artwork, which included the restoration of the striking mosaics by Sir Eduardo Paolozzi RA and the introduction of Daniel Buren's *Diamonds and Circles* – his first permanent public commission in the UK.

Accommodation of large-scale civil and structural engineering allowed for over-site development and facilitated future development of the new Elizabeth line.

Daniel Buren's art installations create a welcoming and dynamic entrance to Tottenham Court Road station and aid wayfinding.

TOTTENHAM COURT ROAD STATION
PRIMARK
READY FOR ADVENTURE.

Paddington Bakerloo Line Station

Westminster, London
Completed 2024

Designed for Sellar Properties, improvements work to the Bakerloo line ticket hall at Paddington Underground station transforms passenger experience and provides a gateway to the wider Paddington Square development.

A significant expansion of the Bakerloo line ticket hall, complete with an increased number of ticket gates, optimizes passenger flow, reduces journey time and alleviates peak-hour congestion.

A legible and well-lit new entrance at the base of the RPBW building provides a seamless transition to the urban realm above, with step-free access and improved signage creating a more inclusive and streamlined journey to and from the platforms below.

The upgrade also includes improved back-of-house facilities for TfL staff and creates a safe and modernized environment for both Bakerloo line passengers and station staff, while retaining the character of the original London Underground station.

The opening of the upgraded Bakerloo line ticket hall was the culmination of more than twelve years of Scott Brownrigg's design services to improve connectivity and accessibility for passengers at Paddington station.

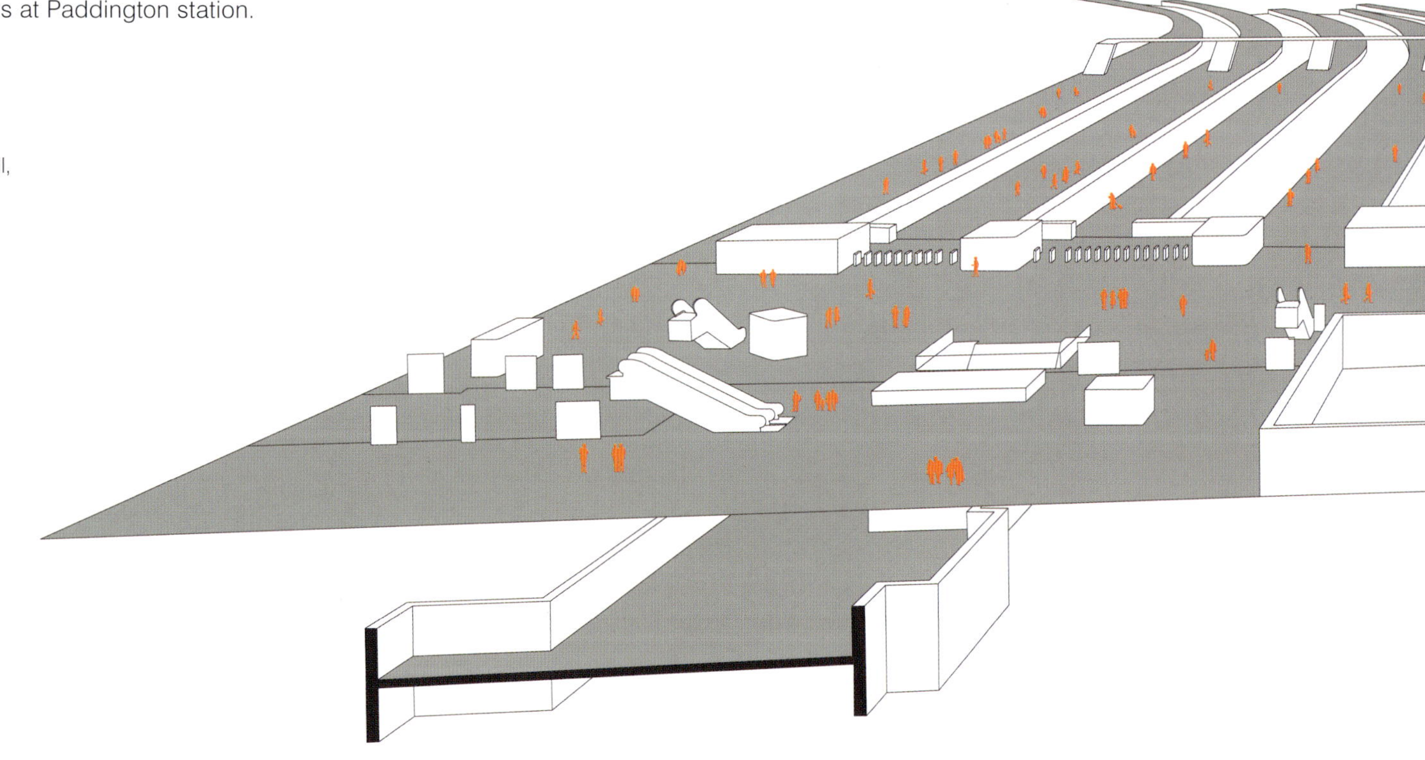

The Paddington Square development, which includes the new Bakerloo line ticket hall, provides a vibrant destination and is the centrepiece of the wider regeneration of the area. Right: Section through the Paddington Square development, with the Paddington Bakerloo line station highlighted orange.

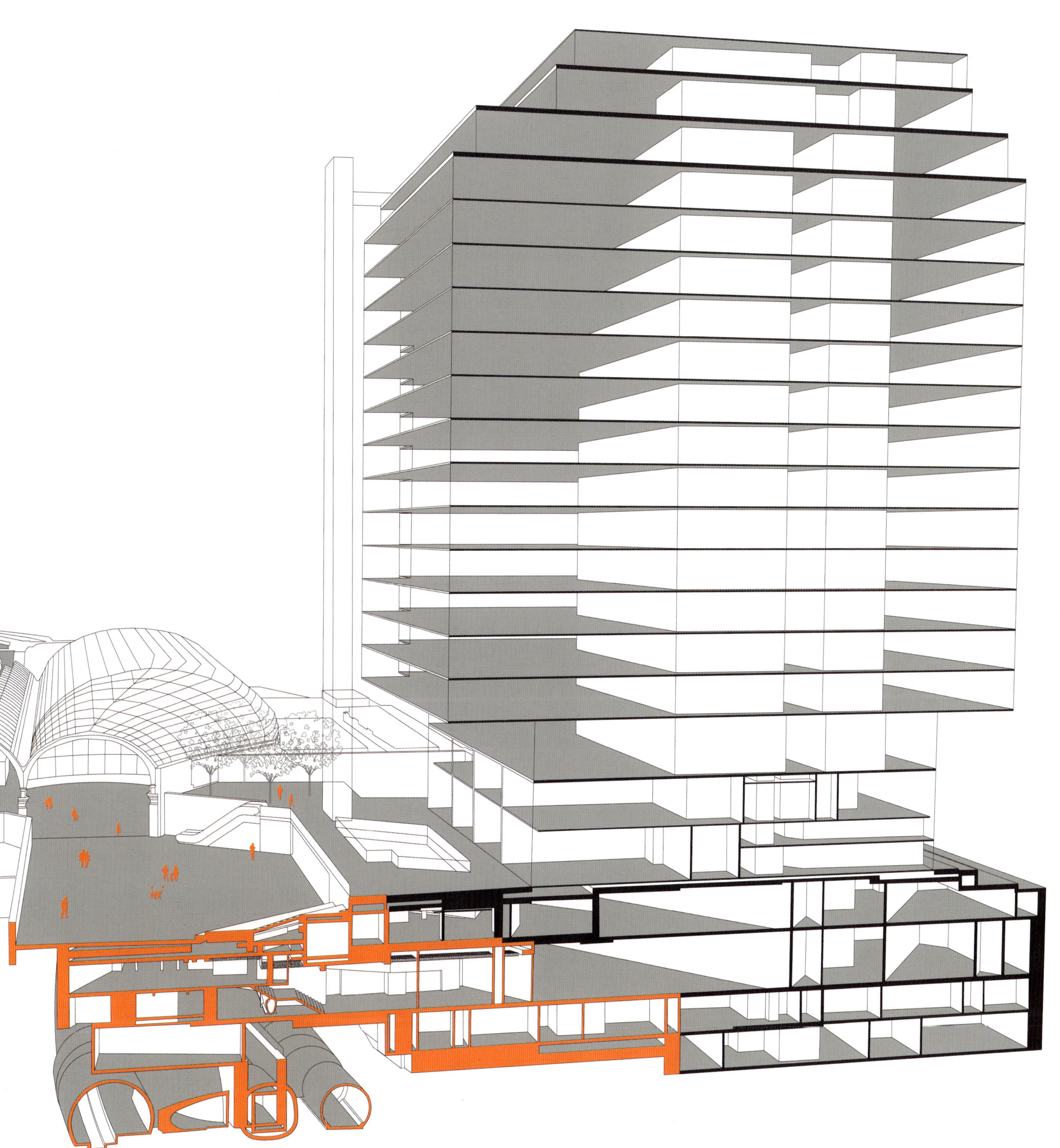

Future Thinking: Rail

Key future trends in transportation design include equity for all, destination places, unlocking of development, and sustainable transport.

The focus on inclusivity and accessibility for all has progressed significantly in the last twenty-five years from the provision of lifts for people using wheelchairs to providing full equity for all transportation users, including those with mobility restrictions, visual or aural impairment, or neurodivergent or neurodegenerative conditions, and both young and ageing populations.

Our goal is to allow people to be able to lead active, engaged and valued lives within their communities. Designing to facilitate people living within their preferred environments, increasing their autonomy, self-confidence and mobility, brings benefits to the whole of society.

The accommodations that allow for the maximum availability of access to public transportation systems offer benefits to everyone. Railway stations should be navigable, open and accepting public spaces that consider the needs of all users, including the operator. Widening station accessibility and usability also improves passenger safety and increases general levels of well-being.

Public railway systems can assist in the reduction of PM2.5 particulates in the areas in which people live, learn, work and socialize. Steel wheel on steel rail produces significantly lower levels of such particulates in the surrounding areas than are produced by personal ICE/EV road vehicles. Increased exposure to PM2.5, in particular, has a major effect on illnesses and morbidity levels in those people who live in such affected areas.

Stations are among the few civic buildings that people use on a daily basis. With its cross-sector experience, Scott Brownrigg is able to develop high-quality mixed-use, transport-orientated communities, creating destinations in places with high and regular footfall. Mass Rapid Transit and Light Rail Transit (LRT) systems help to enable fifteen-minute living for locals. This then allows communities to access such valuable resources as primary healthcare, childcare, employment, working from near home, education, socializing space and retail. The incorporation of destination space widens the appeal and benefit of the station.

There is a symbiotic relationship between transport infrastructure and development, typified by the completion of the Paddington Bakerloo line station scheme as part of the greater Sellar Properties Paddington Square development. Lessons from such cities as Hong Kong and Singapore, where the practice is currently delivering Tavistock MRT station for the Singapore Land Transport Authority, could be more widely incorporated into transportation planning and design in the UK. It seems likely that third-party-funded station improvements will become a more common model in the UK.

The modernization and upgrade of existing stations, including numerous MRT and LRT systems built during the 1970s and '80s, are likely to be key areas of growth. Such projects entail the replacement of architectural elements that have reached the end of their useful life with new architectural finishes, the coordination of service-heavy spaces and the incorporation of inclusive and equitable design alongside the development and delivery of new high-quality stations that are as effective to use as a passenger as they are to work in as the operator.

Working together within multidisciplinary design teams, with joint development of construction methodology, is key to retaining train operations and to reducing disruption to the travelling public.

Defence

Defence, the consideration of national security

Erika Gemmell

Over the years Scott Brownrigg has developed a reputation as a leading defence and security architect, both within the UK and internationally. From the design of the Queen Elizabeth Barracks in Guildford – a depot and training centre for the Women's Royal Army Corps opened by Queen Elizabeth II in 1964 – to significant Ministry of Defence (MoD) work during the 1970s and '90s, both within the UK and overseas, and continuing through to today, its history of work in this sector has been incredibly varied.

In the 1970s the Property Services Agency of the Department of the Environment was responsible for MoD work, which included development plans for Royal Naval Armaments Depots at Plymouth and Portsmouth, and new buildings at Frater and Bedenham Royal Naval Armaments Depots to replace those at Priddy's Hard in Portsmouth. The work involved a substantial reappraisal of ancillary civil engineering and services facilities. New and refurbished buildings, including workshops at Plymouth, would act as prototypes for those at the Portsmouth depot – an early example of utilizing standard designs on the defence estate and a trend that continues to this day.

'Design one, build many' is an appropriate axiom in those cases where repetition can generate best value. The practice has worked on a number of projects – including the Army Basing Programme and the Vehicle Storage and Support Programme at MoD Ashchurch – utilizing template design and repeatable design elements to maximize the benefits of design standardization.

By the mid-1970s, the practice was working overseas, on the Queen's Hill Camp in Hong Kong, 8 kilometres from the Chinese border, and in the 1990s it opened a project office in Ayios Nikolaos Station to support the development of the Sovereign Bases in Cyprus.

The practice's support of UK armed forces based abroad continued, adapting experience gained in the UK to the climate and construction methodologies of the local area. Recent work has focused on critical infrastructure delivery for both the British military and the Foreign, Commonwealth and Development Office (FCDO), designing workplaces specific to the nature of their operations at RAF Akrotiri and Episkopi and in Nicosia.

The defining moment for the practice in the defence sector came in 1993 with the opportunity to carry out the technical design delivery for the collocation of the MoD from a number of sites to a single one in Filton, Bristol. The opportunity was viewed favourably by a board member, who recognized the potential to re-establish the practice as a leading defence architect in the UK. Despite some initial resistance around the boardroom table, the decision was made to 'take a risk' and progress with the project, which later become known as MoD Abbey Wood, home of the procurement organizations Defence Equipment and Support and the Submarine Delivery Agency.

The practice worked under a design-and-build contract with John Mowlem. The fast-track programme enabled the delivery of the first buildings at Abbey Wood in December 1994.

MoD Abbey Wood
Demonstrating the benefits of an integrated architectural, services and structural design strategy, MoD Abbey Wood won numerous awards, including Green Building of the Year in 1997.

PJHQ Northwood
Single living accommodation for military and civilian staff at the Permanent Joint Headquarters in Northwood.

The site – comprising 130,000 square metres of low-energy offices (rated BREEAM Excellent) combined with a conference centre, library, dining facilities, crèche, fitness facilities, energy centre and gatehouse buildings – initially housed 5500 MoD staff, rising to 8500 staff by 2020.

To facilitate effective coordination of on-site information exchange and speed of delivery, a design team of thirty staff was established, along with a project site office for the duration of the detailed design and construction period. The project was heralded in Gavin Turner and Jeremy Myerson's book *New Workspace, New Culture* (1998) as 'the most progressive public sector office complex built in Britain for a generation'. The campus won the 1997 RICS Energy Efficiency Award for its ecological design.

As a result of the entrepreneurial spirit that still drives the practice today, Scott Brownrigg went on to develop a respected reputation in the defence and security sector, taking advantage of numerous opportunities to design and deliver major MoD programmes over the next three decades. Throughout its history in this sector, the key to the practice's success has been the value it places on developing long-term relationships with stakeholders from project inception through to construction, completion and beyond.

From 2003 onwards, Scott Brownrigg supported Aspire Defence in a £8 billion, thirty-five-year private finance initiative (PFI), Project Allenby Connaught (pp. 156–60), to run and redevelop the Army garrisons at Aldershot and across Salisbury Plain. The primary aim of the project was to improve the way soldiers live, work and train – in short, to 'make soldiers' lives better'. Recruitment and retention – ongoing necessities for the British military – were to be achieved through delivery of high-quality, purpose-built and fully serviced living and working accommodation for 18,700 soldiers (over 20 per cent of the British Army). After more than a decade of ongoing successful delivery, the practice was appointed to deliver the Army Basing Programme, which would support the return to Salisbury Plain of troops based in Germany.

To achieve best value and enable speed of delivery, designs for generic building types were developed alongside the design of bespoke buildings, to allow for standardized construction. For example, off-site modular construction was used on the single living accommodation, bringing

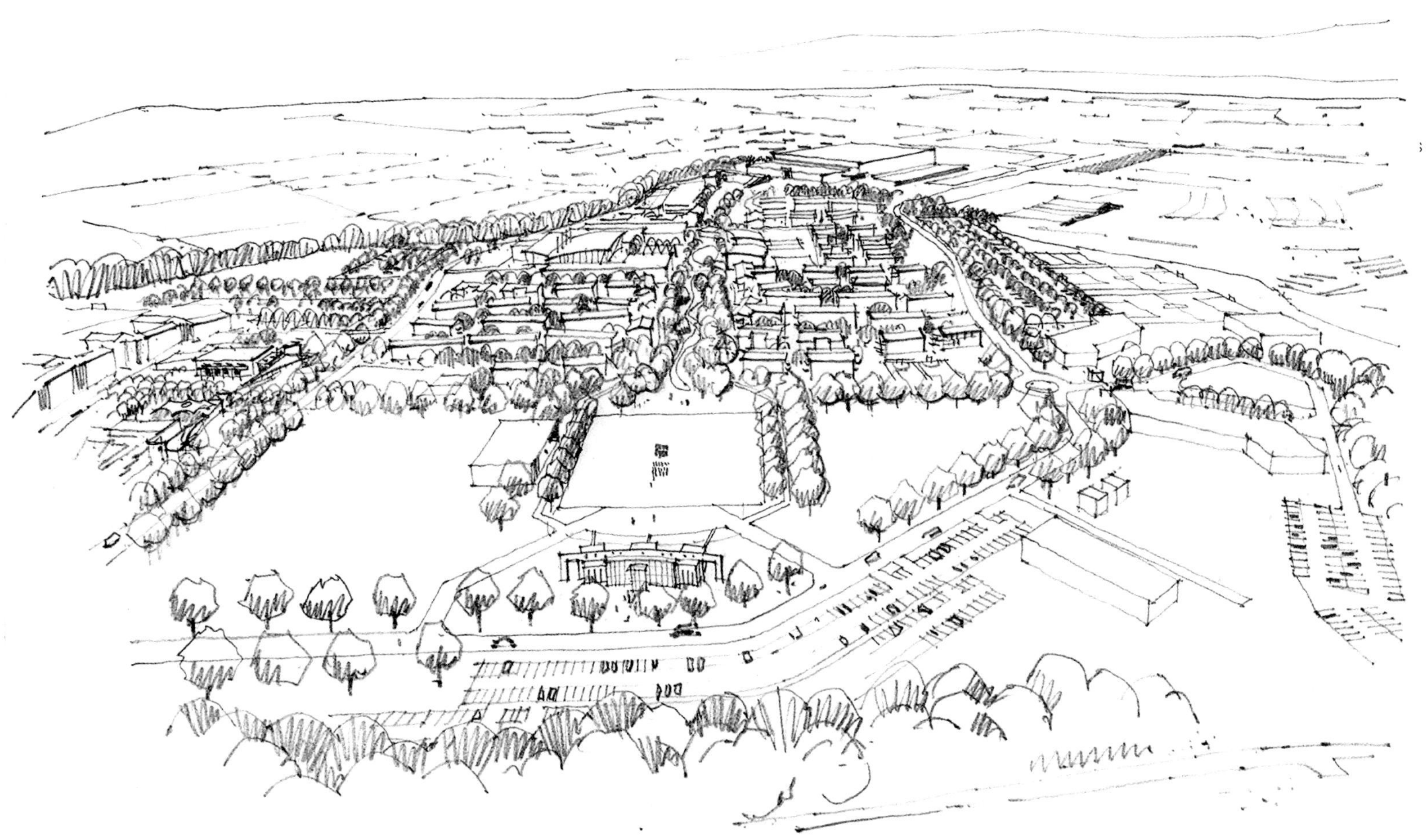

Defence Technical Training College, St Athan
Aerial sketch of the Defence Technical Training College masterplan in St Athan, Wales.

the benefits of programme speed, quality of build and increased construction safety. Component design was utilized to achieve individual buildings of varying sizes while maximizing the benefits of a kit of parts, as in the case of the Junior Ranks Dining Centre in Aldershot.

Where appropriate, specification was standardized across buildings. The lifespan and detailing of products were thoroughly verified to ensure that material selection provided best value and achieved the set design standards agreed between the MoD, facilities management and end users. In 2011 the British Safety Council awarded the project the Sword and Globe of Honour in recognition of a 'safety first always' culture that resulted in a safety performance surpassing the UK construction industry average by a factor of ten.

Building on the Abbey Wood experience of large-scale delivery, the design of secure operational headquarters became a key focus area for the practice, with projects including the Permanent Joint Headquarters at Northwood (pp. 148–51); a Specialist Headquarters at RAF Wyton in Cambridgeshire (pp. 154–55); the Foreign, Commonwealth and Development Office (FCDO) in Buckinghamshire; the Squadron Ops Headquarters at RAF Marham in Norfolk; and the redevelopment of the Surrey Police Headquarters at Mount Browne in Guildford.

Each project is unique, but common to all is a high level of stakeholder engagement and of knowledge of the end users. These qualities have informed the design of bespoke, fully fit-for-purpose, secure infrastructure solutions.

R&D Facility, Luton
The scheme incorporates specialized laboratory, R&D and testing equipment and bespoke features such as a meeting pod suspended within the atrium volume.

Scott Brownrigg's expertise in the design of specialist facilities recognizes ever-demanding security needs, both physical and cyber, while ensuring that the building design focuses on the workplace setting and provision of collaborative and flexible working environments for all personnel.

Following the closure in 2012 of RAF Lyneham in Wiltshire as an active RAF station (the airfield was built in 1939), the MoD looked to redevelop the site as a world-class training establishment for the Army's corps of Royal Electrical and Mechanical Engineers (REME) under the Defence Technical Training Change Programme.

The Lyneham site extended to 466 hectares, comprising a former airfield of approximately 390 hectares and a technical area of around 80 hectares. A comprehensive review of the site was undertaken to determine how best to transform it into a modern training facility. This major project involved the construction and refurbishment of eighty-three assets, as well as the site-wide upgrade of an existing utilities network, all within a tight programme, commencing service in 2015.

MoD Lyneham was born out of the since-halted Defence Technical Training College, a tri-service training facility for the British Armed Forces at

St Athan. The original brief was to rationalize engineering and information systems training facilities for the Army, Navy and RAF into a single college. It was set to be the largest public–private partnership (PPP) project in the UK at the time and the largest single investment in Wales.

At Royal Naval Air Station (RNAS) Yeovilton in Somerset, new training facilities formed part of Project Winfra, which was delivered in 2017. The wider programme provided the estate infrastructure necessary to collocate the Army's Wildcat Force and the Navy's HMA Force, resulting in the creation of a single main operating base for the MoD's new Wildcat helicopter. As well as reflecting the Navy's reputation for delivering world-class training facilities, the programme also ensured significant operational savings. A new-build Aircraft/Amphibious Vehicle Underwater Escape and Survival Training Facility permits life-safety training in a controlled environment. Synthetic training provides an efficient training regime in monitored environments and, combined with the creation of bespoke simulation spaces, enhances the learning experience.

In 2004 the practice completed a purpose-built research and development facility near Luton Airport for a confidential multinational aerospace, defence and information security company. A state-of-the-art laboratory and testing facility features anechoic chambers for acoustic testing, while a separate office building accommodates up to 1000 engineering and support staff. The scheme enhances staff well-being, productivity and security, while enabling the rationalization of system operations. Research and development facilities have also been designed for other key defence suppliers; for example, the National Maritime Systems Centre at Portsdown Technology Park in Portsmouth (completed 2020) is a facility that can exploit emerging technologies at pace.

At MoD Ashchurch in Gloucestershire, ongoing works in the Vehicle Storage and Support Programme provide Controlled Humidity Environment (CHE) storage for over 4000 vehicles and workshops for inspection and maintenance, as well as essential supporting office space for the MoD. The redevelopment of this centralized facility includes thirteen new buildings, each designed to support the government's net zero targets through the use of modern methods of construction, with provision to generate solar energy on-site and achieve a BREEAM Excellent rating. The enhancement of future capability and the reduction of costs through the delivery of a sustainable estate are transforming MoD Ashchurch into a facility that will support, protect and strengthen the operational readiness of the British Army's vehicle and equipment fleet.

Scott Brownrigg has continued to build and diversify its defence and security capability, relishing the challenges of a complex brief and drawing on expertise in other sectors to provide clients with optimum solutions. Ensuring operational capability and delivering a final design solution lie at the heart of its approach, enabling the practice to continue leading, designing and delivering programmes for top-level budget stakeholders around the world.

Permanent Joint Headquarters (PJHQ), Northwood

Northwood, Middlesex
Completed 2010

The Permanent Joint Headquarters is the UK's principal military HQ site and home to five operational HQs: Strategic Command HQ, Standing Joint Force HQ, Permanent Joint Headquarters, the Commander Allied Maritime Command (one of NATO's three major Commanders) and the Royal Navy's Maritime Operations Centre. The site covers 17 hectares in a semi-urban setting. Scott Brownrigg's involvement extended from initial concept in 2005 through to the official opening of the headquarters building by Queen Elizabeth II in 2010 and to remaining support buildings thereafter. The regeneration programme was carried out within tight physical and security constraints, all achieved without off-site relocation of any staff or parking spaces, ensuring logistics were central to design planning.

The masterplan provided a clear framework for rationalizing the diverse activities on the campus. Single living accommodation and a recreational and community hub wrap around a core of operational buildings, with new site access, security control and parking creating a safe, secure and high-quality living and working environment for over 2500 military and civilian staff.

The new 15,000-square-metre headquarters building – the major focal point – provides a modern, flexible and well-serviced open-plan environment, with improved space efficiency and increased comfort and functionality.

The regeneration involved the demolition of a large number of buildings and the construction of new, converted and refurbished facilities, along with the replacement of the site services infrastructure. Mature trees were retained and reinforced with substantial new planting throughout the site.

The design – which achieved a BREEAM Excellent rating – is sensitive to its setting and surroundings, discreetly incorporating effective security and counterterrorist measures and creating distinctive architecture and interiors appropriate to the unique functional requirements.

PJHQ Northwood completed on time and budget to widespread acclaim, with a carefully phased programme of demolition and construction allowing for the maintenance of full operational capability at the heart of what was a complex site regeneration.

A key element of the Ministry of Defence's commitment to achieving improvements in its estate and the conditions in which its personnel live and work was a programme of private finance initiatives, Northwood being one. The project provided a clear illustration of how investment in building infrastructure and the workplace can be used as a catalyst for transformational change and the adoption of new and more effective ways of working.

The PJHQ commands joint and multinational military operations on behalf of the Ministry of Defence.

JOINT HEADQUARTERS
Toilets
Lift
Liaison officers
Mail room
Reprographics dept
Waste management

PJHQ Northwood
Since completion, the Permanent Joint Headquarters has won a number of awards, including the Partnerships Bulletin Award for Best Operational Project in 2011.

JOINT HEADQUARTERS

King's Troop Royal Horse Artillery

Greenwich, London
Completed 2012

Scott Brownrigg's new home for the King's Troop Royal Horse Artillery at Napier Lines, Woolwich, provides an equine complex focused on an elegant but robust and sustainable solution with an exceptional carbon rating.

The challenge was threefold: to accommodate 170 horses and the troop's Second World War gun carriages on a restrictive historic site while reusing and retaining as many buildings as possible – and simultaneously to design a 'carbon-minus' facility (that is, one that creates more energy than it consumes). The strategy was to approach the proposal from a non-doctrinaire viewpoint and to use environmental performance as a key guide to the design.

In addition to the stabling, associated workshops and stores, and provision for the gun carriages, the scheme features an indoor riding school with viewing gallery, a museum, a gun park and regimental offices. Extensive equine training areas with a manège, canter track and forming-up area for the mounted troop and gun carriages are also provided.

The forward-thinking design incorporates various sustainable measures, including solar chimneys for natural stack ventilation of the stables. Most notably, the stable complex uses biofuel made from horse manure and bedding to generate hot water and space heating for the facilities, a groundbreaking innovation of the time.

Sustainability is the driving force behind the development, which achieved a BREEAM Excellent rating on completion.

Project Pride

RAF Wyton,
Huntingdon,
Cambridgeshire
Completed 2013

Under the Programme to Rationalise and Integrate the Defence Intelligence Estate (PRIDE), a new state-of-the-art building with supporting facilities was designed and constructed to house intelligence staff in a completely open-plan environment. The Pathfinder Building, or Defence Intelligence Fusion Centre, provides analysts with the opportunity to work in new collaborative ways and is the first building of its kind in the UK.

Scott Brownrigg designed this secure facility at RAF Wyton in Cambridgeshire to support the MoD's Defence Intelligence Modernisation Programme. The main headquarters facility features a distinctive 70-metre curved roof that provides a highly effective solution to the demanding security and CTM requirements of the project.

Completed in 2013, the development accommodates more than 1100 personnel across the headquarters and several supporting technical buildings, each designed to achieve a BREEAM Excellent rating.

The entrance to the Pathfinder Building at RAF Wyton.

Pathfinder Building

Project Allenby Connaught

Hampshire and Wiltshire
Completed 2014

One simple mission to make life better for some 18,700 soldiers was achieved through the provision of modern, high-quality, purpose-built living and working accommodation. This was accomplished through innovative design solutions that combined clear masterplanning with thoughtful building design at six garrisons, spanning 1240 hectares, in Aldershot and across Salisbury Plain.

For over twenty years Scott Brownrigg led the design on behalf of Aspire Defence through a combination of collaborative working, excellent communication and positive engagement with all stakeholders.

As a result of successful ongoing delivery, a further phase – for the Army Basing Programme – was awarded to the practice in 2015. This phase provided infrastructure for about 4000 extra troops and approximately 1300 service families newly based in the Salisbury Plain area.

A campus approach focused on the delineation of Live, Work and Train environments while creating 'village living' environments with grouped facilities (dining, welfare and sports). Provision of extensive single living accommodation through off-site modular construction – which achieved a BREEAM Excellent rating – assisted the MoD in the delivery of the British Army's recruitment and retention targets and in the attainment of the project vision to 'make soldiers' lives better'.

In 2008 the project received Public Private Finance Awards for Best Operational Defence Scheme and Best Operational UK Project. It also won numerous sustainability and environmental awards.

In the middle of the Tidworth site on Salisbury Plain is a purpose-built Physical and Recreational Training Centre, which features a dramatic curved glulam roof.

Project Allenby Connaught
Masterplan of the Army Basing camp at Tidworth Garrison, Wiltshire.

Project Allenby Connaught
Located next to living accommodation on the Aldershot site, the Junior Ranks Dining Centre provides a place for military and civilian staff to congregate.

Future Thinking: Defence

Scott Brownrigg is supporting the Defence Estate Optimisation Programme, contributing to the Ministry of Defence's strategic review of, and commitment to invest in, key defence sites across the UK. With a focus on enhancing the lives of people and the defence capability that the estate portfolio supports, the programme is addressing the need for facilities to be more efficient and sustainable, and to deliver value by creating lasting benefits.

Design for defence and security is becoming increasingly people-centric, with an emphasis on providing high-quality environments and amenities that can support and enhance operational readiness, well-being and training.

The rationalization and modernization of existing sites – which focus on repurposing and refurbishment, where possible – create opportunities to enhance future capability, reduce operational costs and deliver sustainable objectives. Off-site construction is likely to remain fundamental to delivering the quality and quantity of construction planned for the MoD. Use of volumetric off-site modular steel construction in Scott Brownrigg projects has been a key delivery method for the last twenty years, proving particularly effective for the design of single living accommodation.

The UK government's drive for net-zero carbon emissions is enabling the practice to review designs holistically, with opportunities to deliver linked renewable-energy facilities. Sustainability was the driving force behind the 2012 scheme for the King's Troop Royal Horse Artillery's new carbon-minus home at Napier Lines, Woolwich. Setting a benchmark in sustainable design, the innovative approach has since driven the aspiration to achieve net-zero carbon across the defence sector, and has been widely adopted in the design of individual buildings, as well as in estate-wide schemes.

Education

Education for all: inspirational places to learn and grow

Ian Pratt and Helen Taylor

Scott Brownrigg's approach to education projects puts people at the heart of the design process, creating inclusive places that everyone can enjoy confidently and independently, with choice and dignity; transformational spaces that nurture and improve educational outcomes, are sustainable and well connected, and have the capacity to evolve.

Peterborough County School for Girls in Cambridgeshire was one of the practice's founding projects, won by Annesley Brownrigg in 1910 in competition against 107 other architects. Four post-war schools for Ilford followed, along with extensions to Reed's School, Cobham – including boarding houses opened in 1959 by Queen Elizabeth, The Queen Mother – and Tillingbourne School in Chilworth.

The practice would go on to work on projects around the world for learners of all ages; projects encompassing a wide variety of providers, institutions, educational models, curricula and special needs, and with design opportunities and experience spanning estate strategy development, campus masterplanning, urban design, new-build development, reuse, adaptation and conservation of existing buildings.

In 1976 John Brownrigg provided consultancy work for the Ministry of Education in Tanzania and in the following year wrote the report *Primary Schools for Tanzania: Universal Primary Education – School Buildings and Equipment*. Other than some dated references to the value of asbestos, this report reflects many of the challenges and opportunities that arise in connection with today's education projects, among them the value of local community support; the benefits of simple design approaches and centralized standards, and of off-site construction balanced against the importance of local and natural materials; and the societal requirement for skills to be taught in a school setting.

Education environments in any setting reflect their social, environmental and political context. John Brownrigg's research also created a rich seam of research reports, publications and technical advisory work in the sector that continues to this day.

In the UK, Scott Brownrigg has contributed to all recent government education building initiatives, including the School Rebuilding Programme, the Priority School Building Programme, Building Schools for the Future (BSF), the Learning and Skills Council Capital Programme and projects procured under the private finance initiative (PFI) and public–private partnership (PPP) programmes and, most recently, the Mutual Investment Model. Work also includes industry-leading research and the preparation of design guidance to support enhancement and sustainability of the education estate.

A defining moment that led to the expansion of the education sector within the practice was winning the Kent Schools PFI project in 2004 and designing six secondary schools for Kent County Council (KCC) – Holmesdale in Snodland, The Malling in East Malling, Aylesford School Sports College, Ellington School for Girls in Ramsgate, The North School in Ashford and Hugh Christie Technology College in Tonbridge – with a combined construction value of £93 million. At the time, the practice had not been involved in school design for a considerable period of time, so it had to find an approach that would embrace its experience of other sectors in order to discover a new way of delivering education. As in the case of the defence sector, the notion of re-entering the education sector was initially not universally supported, but the CEO believed it was a sector in which Scott Brownrigg had a responsibility to deploy its skills, and he enlisted specialist help from an experienced education architect (who later became Managing Director) to explore a fresh new approach.

A key aim was to transform school efficiency. Drawing on experience in a range of sectors, the practice's designs reduced typical travel distances between key learning spaces in order to maximize curriculum delivery, while also introducing internal congregation spaces. In creating new approaches

Kent Schools
Kent Schools were designed using a kit-of-parts approach that was adapted and delivered across six sites; The North School in Ashford is shown here.

to school design, the practice was able to support evolving learning and teaching methods. While driving through the countryside on his way to the presentation to KCC, the CEO, Darren Comber, noted numerous converted barns. Originally built for agricultural use, they had been repurposed as places to live. Comber coined the term 'learning barn' to encapsulate the principles of this innovative education environment; it is a term that has since been widely adopted by the sector.

The simple and cost-effective designs maximized the potential for off-site fabrication and design standardization, while a limited palette of materials and components maximized economies of scale to streamline the building process. The dramatic use of external canopies to link individual learning barns proved popular with the schools and was praised by the Commission for Architecture and the Built Environment, the powerful government design guardian of the time.

Aylesford School Sports College was officially opened on 28 May 2008 by the Secretary of State for Children, Schools and Families, Ed Balls, accompanied by local MP Jonathan Shaw and officials from KCC. Referring to Aylesford School, together with The Malling and Holmesdale, the minister said: 'If we can do around the country, what we've seen in these three schools, we could really transform education in Britain.'

The 'learning barn' typology was adopted beyond Kent, including in the design for Ruislip High School in Hillingdon, London, which completed in 2007 and subsequently achieved fame as the fictional Rudge Park Comprehensive in the Channel 4 TV series *The Inbetweeners*.

The intense focus on the sector in 2004 arose from the Labour government's new BSF investment programme, which was intended to transform the school estate and education experience of young people. Scott Brownrigg's involvement in the programme began with Newham BSF in London, with the design and delivery of Rokeby Boys' School in Canning Town and Sarah Bonnell School for Girls in Stratford. The latter, completed in 2010, was heavily influenced by the dominant form of the retained Edwardian Board School building. It carefully integrated the new with the old and provided facilities that could be used by the community. In 2011 the school was highly commended in the Healthy Schools category of the Best of British Schools Awards of the British Council for School Environments, for excellence in the provision of dining or outdoor play facilities.

Education buildings form an important part of our social infrastructure, and many of the practice's education designs have included the provision of facilities shared by the local community. Chilton Trinity Technology College in Bridgwater, part of Somerset BSF, included a shared leisure centre with a 25-metre swimming and learner pool. One of the practice's most impactful projects during this period was the UK's first Parent Promoted School, The Elmgreen School in London (pp. 172–73), completed in 2009 as part of the award-winning Lambeth BSF programme.

Shortly after completion of The Elmgreen School, the practice designed St Bartholomew's School in Newbury – part of West Berkshire Council's BSF pilot programme and procured via the Improvement and Efficiency South East framework. The school was one of the few in England at the time to achieve a BREEAM Excellent rating at both pre- and post-construction stages. The design concept draws on natural themes, with the plan form being analogous to a flower – five petals arranged around a stamen. The central hub, with a 1000-square-metre tensile fabric roof, provides a stimulating inside–outside environment that can be used year-round. In 2011 St Bartholomew's won the prestigious Green Apple Award, presented to organizations showcasing exceptional sustainability initiatives and environmental best practice.

Three Rivers Academy
The 1875-pupil school is an example of a new state school building procured outside the Education and Skills Funding Agency (ESFA) Contractors Framework.

Two years later, Coleg Cymunedol Y Dderwen (Gateway to the Valleys) Comprehensive School in Bridgend completed. It is believed to have been the first UK school of its type to achieve a BREEAM Outstanding rating both pre- and post-construction. It won the 2013 BREEAM Education Award and became an exemplar project for Constructing Excellence in Wales and the Low Carbon Research Institute.

Undertaken in parallel with the BSF projects, South Thames College in Wandsworth was one of a number of major part refurbishment, part new-build further education schemes progressed by the practice. It was funded by the Learning and Skills Council and completed in 2010 while the college retained occupation of the adjoining Grade II-listed building.

The Academies Programme, introduced in March 2000, initially targeted 'failing' schools but was subsequently expanded to include a variety of school types independent of local authority control and funded directly by the Department for Education (DfE). The programme led to the successful design and delivery of several academies, including Maltings Academy and New Rickstones Academy in Witham, Essex, in 2012; Winterbourne Academy in South Gloucestershire in 2014; and Three Rivers Academy in Hersham, Surrey, in 2018 (pp. 184–87). Merchants' Academy Primary School and Venturers' Academy in Bristol (completed 2021) also provided opportunities to design bespoke accommodation for pupils with special educational needs.

Particularly of note was Harris Invictus Academy in Croydon, which completed in 2017 and won Project of the Year at the 2018 Education Estates Awards. The project was conceived by the grass roots community group Invictus and procured in partnership with the Harris Federation. The practice was challenged to create a vibrant, secure learning environment with civic qualities and community access on a compact site in London Road that

Harris Invictus Academy
Community spaces activate the street at ground level, while the vertical brise-soleil offers controlled views in and out of the learning spaces above.

had been extensively damaged in the riots of 2012. The development of the brief and design for this new free school involved extensive engagement with the stakeholders. A strong street presence and an active frontage were required for the urban context. Sports facilities needed to be easily accessed out of hours by local residents and clubs. These included a multi-use games area, sports pitches and an external play space located at the rear of the site.

This period saw significant change in government funding and standards in the UK education sector. In 2008, a year before The Elmgreen School completed, the UK economy was hit by the global banking crisis. And in 2010 the newly elected Conservative–Liberal Democrat coalition government ended BSF. While Local Education Partnerships continued to progress established BSF projects, public investment was greatly reduced or cancelled completely. Nevertheless, it was acknowledged that continued investment was required to deal with an ageing school estate, rising birth rates and the need continually to improve educational experiences and outcomes.

Sebastian James, CEO of the retailer Dixons Carphone, led a major review panel tasked with considering the existing DfE capital expenditure and with making recommendations for future delivery models for capital investment in schools. The review of BSF identified successes but also evidence of a cumbersome procurement process. The result was a challenge to design and construct 'more for less'. In collaboration with school building framework contractor Galliford Try and engineer Max Fordham, and with significant input from an expert advisory group of headteachers, Scott Brownrigg's Optimum Schools model responded with a creative design solution, delivering reduced floor area without loss of teaching space, flexibility on a day-to-day basis and adaptability for future growth or change of use, robust specification, simplified building services, ease of operation and reduced running costs.

Simplicity of form was essential in striving for an elegant solution, leading to simplicity of construction in order to optimize limited funding. The form echoed a child's view of what a house might look like: symmetrical, familiar and functional, but with the opportunity for exciting spaces under a dual-pitched roof. A predominantly off-site-manufactured kit-of-parts solution embedded the economic benefits of standardization while acknowledging that every site and school is different. All teaching spaces were dual-aspect and were clustered around a hub space for breakout teaching. The externalization of a large proportion of circulation space allowed for required area reductions without sacrificing valuable internal learning space.

Hillview School for Girls in Tonbridge, Kent, became the first to apply the Optimum Schools approach. The school was looking not only to replace tired temporary buildings, but also to use new spaces as a vehicle to challenge and develop its pedagogical approach, which was exploring new ways of teaching science influenced by Project Faraday. Completed in 2014, the Hillview addition was built in just twenty-one weeks. Feedback was overwhelmingly positive; one student suggested that 'the building smiles'. The teachers were delighted with the new and alternative learning spaces, which allowed them to develop more forward-thinking methods of teaching.

The approach was subsequently applied to the Hub South East Scotland framework in the Lothians and Edinburgh. The practice completed a total of forty-six 'Rising Rolls' school buildings, ranging in value from £2 million to £6 million. In tandem, Optimum was adopted for eight schools (valued at £35 million and completed in 2016) as part of the new DfE Priority School Building Programme in North and Northeast Lincolnshire.

Ditton Park Academy in Slough, one of a new breed of independently managed, state-funded 'free schools' in England', was also one of the first secondary school projects to be completed using the Optimum Schools principles. It won the Innovation in Delivering Value category at the Education Estates Awards in 2018.

As part of the free schools programme, University Technical Colleges (UTCs) were established to offer technically orientated courses that combined National Curriculum requirements with technical and vocational elements for students aged between fourteen and eighteen. Designed to prepare students for careers in science, technology, engineering and mathematics, Scott Brownrigg projects included Sir Charles Kao UTC in Harlow, Essex (completed 2014; now known as BMAT STEM Academy), which features spaces to support the Conceive, Design, Implement, Operate (CDIO) educational framework.

UTC Swindon, also completed in 2014, is an award-winning conversion of the Grade II-listed Great Western Railway School and a former fire station and mill building. The scheme involved extensive engagement with UTC sponsors Oxford Brookes University and Johnson Matthey, along with Swindon Borough Council, English Heritage and the local community. The concept celebrated the link between 'historic' engineering and 'engineering the future', creating innovative, inspirational facilities while also protecting and enhancing the retained buildings and structures, which are part of the historic Swindon Railway Village. A central, new-build element connects the existing buildings and takes inspiration from the former smithy. Glass and weathering steel distinguish this structure from the historic stone-built ones.

Mulberry UTC, built on the constrained high-street site of the former Bow Fire Station in east London, specializes in the creative and health industries. Completed in 2017, its facilities include

Hitchen Centre, North Hertfordshire College
The scheme revives the Hitchin Centre through the refurbishment of three teaching accommodation blocks and the creation of a new internal 'hub' space.

a purpose-built, 250-seat theatre designed with the National Theatre, media suites, theatre-set construction and costume workshops, and hospital and healthcare simulation spaces.

For London Design and Engineering UTC, also completed in 2017, the practice developed the brief and design in consultation with project sponsors the University of East London, Thames Water, Costain, Thames Tideway Tunnel, Newham Borough Council, ABP, London City Airport and the Royal Albert Dock Trust. The design incorporates a new, publicly accessible square and reveals activities taking place in the specialist laboratories to passers-by. Work on a new extension, begun in 2023, is testament to the success of the institution and the strong relationship established by the practice.

Understanding both the educational vision and the business model is key. For providers of further and higher education, architectural vision can inform and transform strategic development plans. The physical estate is one of the largest overheads for any institution; however, facilities can also be used to generate value and create community connections.

University of Reading Malaysia
The design provides a series of flexible teaching spaces alongside fully equipped laboratories, a learning resource centre and four lecture theatres.

Commencing in 2009, the practice conducted a strategic property review and prepared a ten-year architectural estate strategy and masterplan for North Hertfordshire College (pp. 174–75). This work led to a range of completed projects, including the Stevenage and Letchworth Studio Schools and the award-winning Hitchin Centre, demonstrating how strategic architectural interventions can resolve complicated problems.

Long-term collaboration with the University of Reading since 2010 has maximized the value of its estate through the pursuit of planning consents for new development and the delivery of new facilities on a consolidated campus. A new Science and Innovation Park and five sites for residential development allowed funds to be released to further the education investment programme, benefiting the university, its students and the wider community. This long-standing relationship enabled the practice to translate and capture the essence of the UK campus in its design for the university's first overseas campus in Asia – the University of Reading Malaysia (pp. 176–79).

Other notable university projects include work for the University of Westminster (completed 2002); a new media arts centre for the University of Luton (2003); a student reception and residence building, rated BREEAM Excellent, for the University of Surrey (2012); Lancaster University Library Extension (2021); and projects for Newcastle University in Singapore (2017) and Malaysia (2018). Work with Southampton Solent University included its campus masterplan and The Spark (pp. 180–83), an award-winning academic hub and showcase for excellence in learning, teaching, innovation and student achievement that has become the image of the university.

The evolving themes of placemaking, sustainability and student well-being have been a constant thread throughout Scott Brownrigg's work in education – a thread particularly visible in projects for Aberdeen City Council's five-year Capital Programme. The brief for two sister

LEH Foshan, China
Surrounded by high-rise buildings, the design creates an oasis-like campus in the heart of the city where students can live, learn, socialize and participate in sports.

primary schools in Aberdeen, Stoneywood and Milltimber (pp. 188–89), was to design state-of-the-art, two-stream facilities with modern, healthy learning and working environments, conceived around strong sustainable-design and placemaking principles. Both have been recognized across the industry, with numerous award shortlistings and wins, including the Learning Places Scotland Awards, the Scottish Design Awards and the Aberdeen Society of Architects Awards. These projects – together with New City College's Epping Forest Wellness Centre in Debden, Essex (completed 2024) – feature expressed engineered-timber structures, which offer substantial reductions in embodied carbon compared with other materials and – drawing on biophilic design principles – contribute to healthier learning environments.

Across this history of work in education, the private independent schools sector has broadened opportunities for Scott Brownrigg, both in the UK – with such award-winning innovative projects as the Activity Centre at St George's College in Weybridge (pp. 190–93) – and internationally, where a long-term relationship with the high-performing Lady Eleanor Holles (LEH) School in Hampton resulted in the practice's first overseas international school. Located in China, LEH Foshan completed in 2021. Education work continues to grow in the UK and worldwide, with concepts and strategic advisory services delivered for forty-two schools in Oman; 2500 student accommodation places for Khalifa University in Abu Dhabi; and the shortlisting of the Island Private School in Limassol, Cyprus, in the Future Projects category at the World Architecture Festival Awards in 2024.

The Elmgreen School

Lambeth, London
Completed 2009

The Elmgreen School in Tulse Hill was the first Parent Promoted School in the UK and part of the award-winning Lambeth Building Schools for the Future programme.

Designed to provide places for 1100 students aged between eleven and eighteen, the concept – which was developed in collaboration with a wide range of stakeholders – was to create a single-envelope building with accommodation arranged around a large central space based on the idea of a medieval market square.

Enclosed by a 'sawtooth' roof with extensive glazing, the 'market square' connects the different learning areas and serves as a recreational, social learning and assembly space suitable for community events.

Overarching design objectives included supporting new ways of learning, greater and extended use of technology, increased levels of student autonomy and personalization of the curriculum.

Key features include a rooftop science garden, a hearing-impaired unit, a wide variety of open-plan and reconfigurable spaces and unusually high levels of visibility between spaces, enabling very good natural supervision.

Among the educational benefits attributed to the design by school staff during the first year of operation was a significant improvement against key performance indicators, including a reported 80 per cent reduction in fixed-term exclusions.

The 'market square' is designed to support a range of activities, from individual study and reflection to group discussion, role play and assembly. Below: Section through the 'market square'.

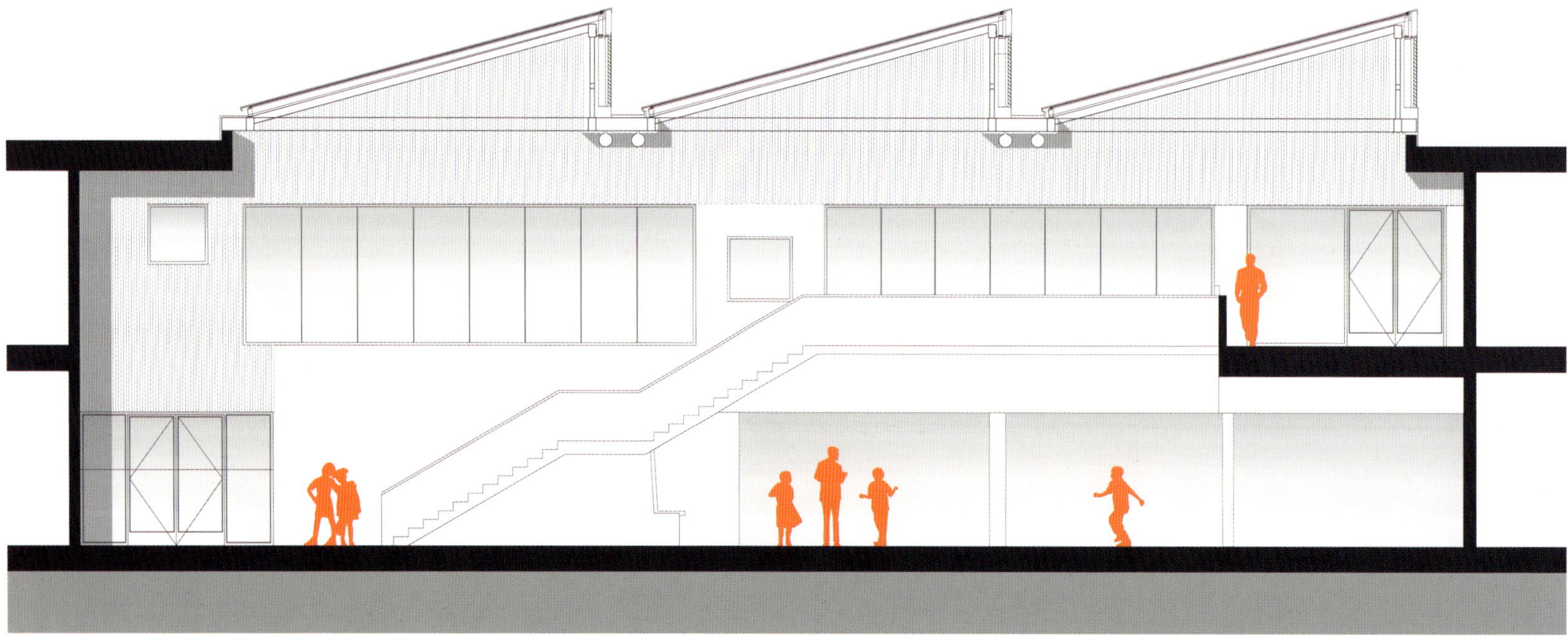

North Hertfordshire College

Stevenage,
Letchworth and
Hitchin, Hertfordshire
Completed 2014

The new and refurbished buildings have transformed the Hitchin campus (left) to reflect the needs of the students, providing sought-after additional areas for learning and social interaction. Pictured below is the entrance to the Da Vinci Studio School of Science and Engineering, now the Stevenage campus of North Hertfordshire College.

The practice's work with North Hertfordshire College began with a strategic property review and preparation of a ten-year architectural estate strategy with masterplan, and culminated in the creation of Stevenage Studio School, Letchworth Studio School and the award-winning Hitchin Centre.

Extensive engagement with college stakeholders was key and resulted in a deep understanding of the educational vision and core values underpinning curriculum delivery, along with current and future space needs. This informed the design vision and strategies underpinning the reimagination and rationalization of the college's estate.

At Hitchin, the practice remodelled and retrofitted three 1960s buildings and enclosed a disused courtyard to create a vibrant new 'hub' surrounded by a range of agile, open-plan learning spaces to support the college's curriculum based on theoretical learning and practical skills.

The structural and cellular nature of the existing buildings presented significant challenges that required imaginative design solutions. Notable examples include the new link bridges, lift and stairs within the main 'hub' space, which stabilize the existing buildings and provide level access to the various floor levels.

Compared with the new-build approach originally contemplated by the college, retaining and upgrading the existing concrete-framed buildings yielded significant environmental and economic benefits.

University of Reading Malaysia

Iskandar Puteri,
Malaysia
Completed 2015

The University of Reading Malaysia, in the state of Johor, is part of EduCity Iskandar – Asia's first multi-institutional education campus – and part of Iskandar Puteri, which is the largest urban integrated development in Southeast Asia.

This was Reading's first campus in Asia, and a key design objective was to capture and translate the essence of the university's UK campus.

The 30,000-square-metre development provides a mixed economy of office and general and specialist teaching facilities, including pharmacy and chemistry labs, for 2000 students and 400 staff in the departments of Law, Business (including the Henley Business School), the Built Environment, Chemistry and Pharmacy.

The accommodation is arranged around a covered heart-space, which blurs the traditional boundaries between buildings and landscape, student areas and staff areas, formal and informal, learning spaces and social spaces. A translucent roof protects the heart-space from direct sunlight and rain, forming a lush green environment for people to work, learn and socialize in. Diagonal ramps at ground level and upper-floor-level bridges cross the heart-space, connecting the two main blocks of accommodation.

The environmentally responsive design was realized through an exemplary briefing and design process led from the UK, with construction-monitoring services provided from Singapore.

Diagonal ramps that cross and define the heart-space are echoed by suspended bridges above that connect the parallel teaching wings.

University of Reading Malaysia
Inspired by traditional Malay houses, the building is lifted off the ground to encourage airflow and natural cooling. Perforated metal veils screening the facades help to limit solar heat gain.

The Spark, Southampton Solent University

Southampton
Completed 2016

Completion of The Spark in May 2016 marked the culmination of a four-year journey to inform, design and deliver Southampton Solent University's vision for teaching and learning on its city-centre campus.

This £33 million project was conceived as an academic hub and a showcase for innovation and achievement. It was also a vehicle for institutional change, and has transformed the Solent experience, helping to achieve major pedagogical enhancements and revolutionizing space utilization monitoring and management.

The design resolved major level differences to facilitate comprehensive barrier-free access to the new and existing facilities. A total of 10,000 square metres of formal and informal space for learning, teaching, work and play forms around an impressive atrium gathering space with a 'Solent Red' Pod at its centre, promoting interdisciplinary activity and interaction between students, academics and visitors. Inspired by Solent's former spark logo and what it symbolizes, the Pod has helped to define and reinforce the university's brand and profile, capturing the interest and imagination of staff, students and the wider community, and attracting students from the UK and overseas.

The game-changing Spark building has also reinvigorated university engagement with employers and wider community engagement, and has given staff and students new ways to see and share their learning and teaching experiences, knowledge and research.

Floor-to-ceiling windows provide a sense of openness, revealing movement and activity, and creating a strong visual connection between building users within and the wider public without. Below: Model section showing the atrium space and the Pod.

The scheme is characterized by bold use of colour and a series of mono-pitched roofs that serve as a contemporary reference to terraced housing on a residential street.

Three Rivers Academy
A concrete structural frame featuring an integrated slab-and-beam design minimizes the columns required and facilitates clear spans across the 'mall' space.

Stoneywood and Milltimber Schools

Aberdeen
Completed
2018 and 2022

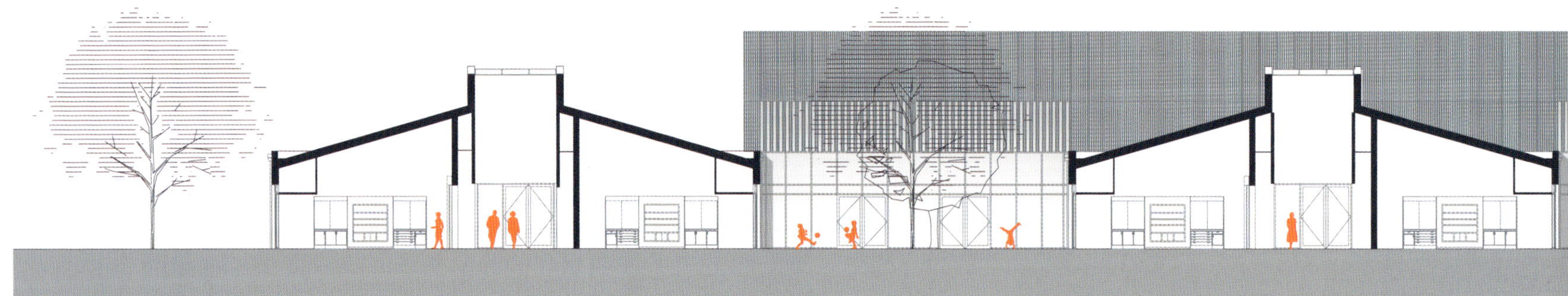

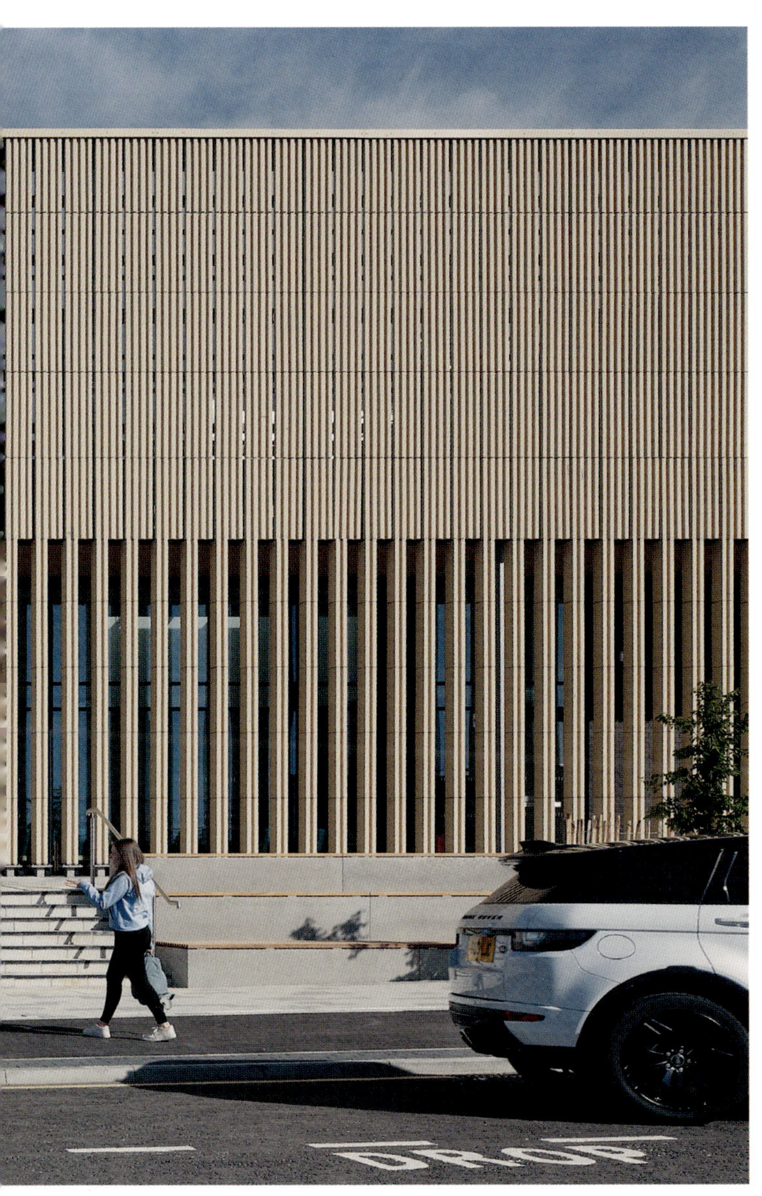

Milltimber School
Milltimber School forms part of the Education New Build Programme, which contributes to Aberdeen City Council's Learning and Childcare Expansion Programme.
Below: Section through classrooms at Milltimber School.

These facilities are a pair of award-winning, highly sustainable, two-stream primary schools with nurseries, designed for Aberdeen City Council and procured under traditional building contracts.

Stoneywood School, which completed in 2018, is located on the site of the former Bankhead Academy to the northwest of the city centre, and Milltimber School, which completed in 2022, is to the southwest of the city, adjacent to a large residential development.

The designs, which were conceived around strong sustainability and placemaking principles, share compositional elements and feature cross-laminated-timber structures chosen for their attractive aesthetic, durability and environmental credentials.

Stoneywood comprises four 'lantern' teaching pavilions arranged around the main assembly spaces. Each pavilion is generated around a spacious, top-lit collaborative activity area encircled by classrooms with direct access to the outdoor learning environment.

At Milltimber, the four teaching pavilions are arranged along a linear circulation route, and the main assembly spaces are on the opposite side of the school, where they form a formal frontage to the public realm.

Both schools feature enhanced outdoor play spaces and PE facilities, promoting health, fitness and well-being, as well as providing improved opportunities for outdoor curricular learning and social interaction.

At the date of completion, Stoneywood was one of the largest cross-laminated-timber education buildings in Scotland.

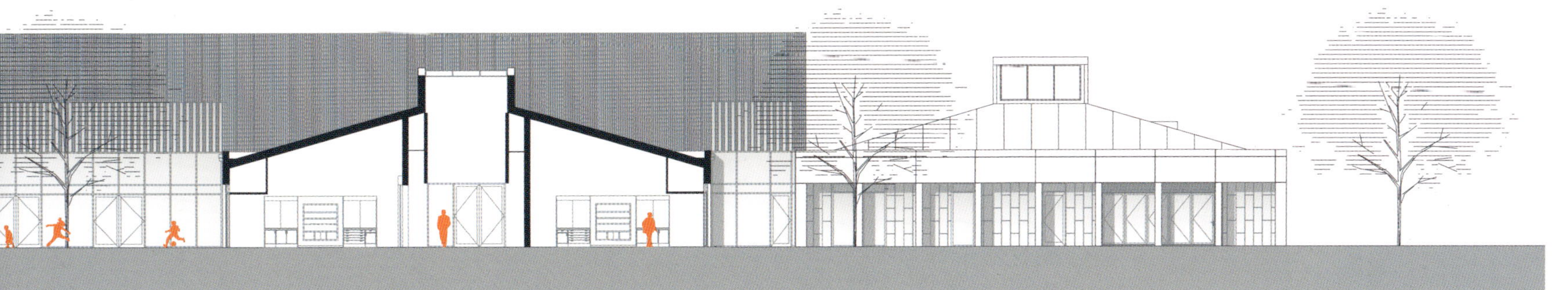

Activity Centre, St George's College

Weybridge, Surrey
Completed 2019

A transformational development designed to deliver 'activity for all', the Activity Centre at St George's College was one of the first projects realized by the practice using parametric modelling and virtual reality.

This exceptional facility, on the college's Grade II-listed park campus in the Weybridge green belt, comprises a six-court sports hall, climbing wall, large fitness suite, dance studio, changing facilities and multi-use spaces for assembly and group activities, including match teas.

Defining features include the undulating roof with an expressed timber structure, which unites the large-volume spaces and blends the building into the landscape, pushing down to denote the main entrance and pulling up to frame views of the outdoor athletics track.

Processional stairs, inspired by the Chapter House stairs at Wells Cathedral, rise from the main entrance and connect the lower campus level with the upper-level athletics track outside. Glazing beside the stairs reveals activities within the primary spaces.

Unusually, the sports hall features a glass sprung floor – the largest of its kind in the UK at completion – with fully programmable LED line markings for a variety of sports. This technology avoids the visual confusion associated with traditional painted line markings.

Use of engineered timber, natural ventilation and on-site renewables helped to make this one of the most sustainable new-build projects delivered by the practice to date.

The Activity Centre, which replaces a 1980s prefabricated building, supports the school's sporting vision and provides an inspirational environment for student and community engagement. Opposite: Section through the Activity Centre.

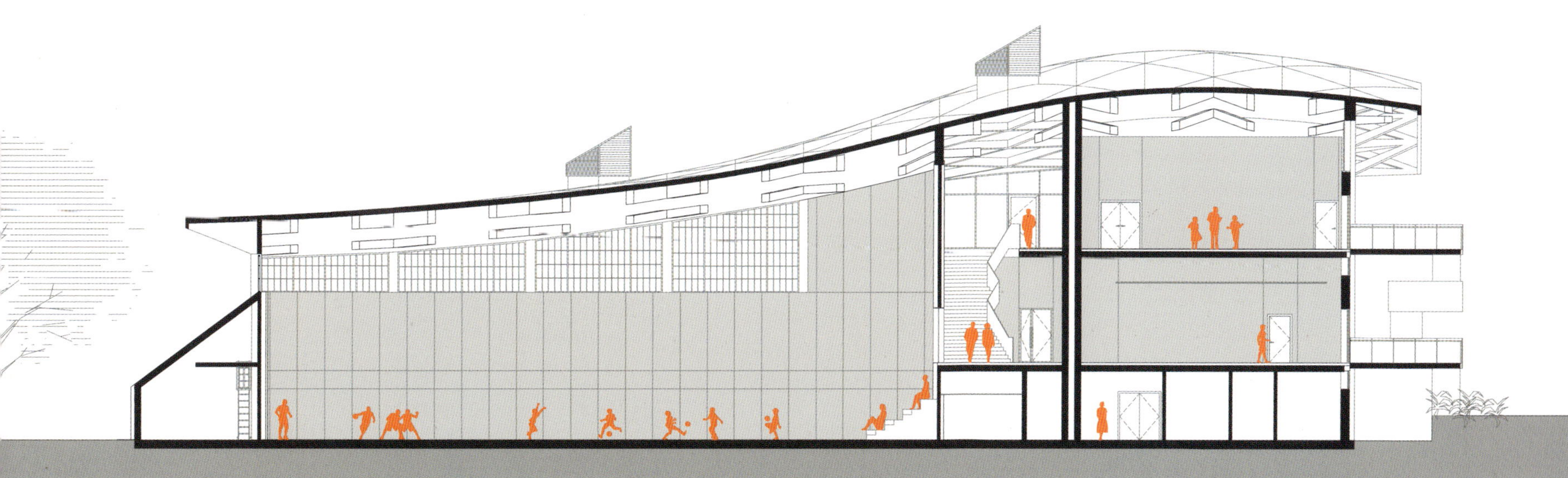

Activity Centre, St George's College
Almost all internal spaces are designed to provide exposure to timber, creating a calming connection to nature and the surrounding woodland.

Future Thinking: Education

The design of education environments ideally supports both delivery of the curriculum and the development of positive life skills that people need in order to flourish in their lives, particularly before the age of twenty-five, when the brain and body are still growing.

According to Teach the Future – a campaign by students to embed climate change in the curriculum – the UK education system should be reformed around climate justice, the natural world and sustainability. The need to address building performance and energy use is already reflected in updates to Department for Education technical standards. The opportunity for schools and colleges to contribute positively to our connection with the natural world, biodiversity net gain and climate adaptation and resilience is reflected in such recent initiatives as the National Education Nature Park and the research that Scott Brownrigg has been appointed to undertake for Natural England on 'Community Access to School and College Grounds'.

This focus on the outdoor environment for learning has increased worldwide since the Covid-19 pandemic, and is reflected in the inspiring brief provided by the Island Private School in Cyprus, which calls for a learning environment that nurtures global citizens with real connections to the natural world. These principles can be applied to wider learning environments, as demonstrated by Scott Brownrigg's competition design for a new headquarters for the Scout Association at Gilwell Park in Epping Forest. Providing opportunities for Scouts to cook, create and have fun, the curved scheme and winding pathways through the parkland setting create a 'journey' of discovery and promote interaction with the natural world.

Many authorities are seeking ways to optimize investment and bring together services. While this 'place-based' approach may be driven by managing budgets and addressing social, education and health issues in their area, it also offers a critical opportunity to address staff and student well-being. Schools and colleges themselves identify student behaviour and teacher recruitment and retention as significant concerns. An attractive, functional, inclusive learning environment, shared with the wider community, is seen as an effective way to start addressing such problems.

These two challenges – of student mental health and behaviour, and of the recruitment of teachers – are also leading to innovation and new digital hybrid teaching methods, which are seeing the emergence of changing building needs. A number of fully online schools have sprung up for young people who are struggling to attend in person owing to health or location barriers. The concept of 'hybrid education' is also now well established as a means of sharing specialist teaching resources across more than one school, and as a useful way of capturing and recording lessons or lectures to be able to rewatch or share beyond the classroom. While this approach creates some challenges for teachers in terms of media skills, building relationships with their students and monitoring progress, it also requires a different kind of teaching and learning environment, one with an even greater focus on digital technology, lighting and acoustics.

International schools are already addressing these challenges, sometimes because of limited pupil numbers in remote locations. They are also often having to work with existing and multistorey environments. While the pandemic caused many people to re-evaluate their lives and leave cities in the UK, cities around the world are still growing and developing, and are in need of new school places. Education institutions are adapting their teaching and learning methods, as well as their curricula, to meet local needs with available accommodation.

This post-pandemic change has also resulted in an opportunity to repurpose existing spaces – creating the potential to mitigate embodied carbon – as well as to breathe new life into existing environments and buildings. Existing mainstream schools in city centres are struggling or closing owing to lack of demand for places, while the need for nursery and special educational needs (SEN) places is growing. The two issues do not always align in terms of location, so that one cannot address the other. The rise in remote working and in different needs of businesses and employees, as well as the changing economy of the high street, has also created an interesting opportunity to relocate educational uses into former commercial spaces. Education facilities bring footfall, which could revitalize a high street, while out-of-town business parks might provide suitable infrastructure, transport connectivity and indoor and outdoor space to meet the needs of students with a range of educational needs or disabilities.

While an individual general classroom or lecture hall might still have the same characteristics as a Victorian school, every other space within the education setting – inside and out – is changing. The typical idea of a school or college building on its own site, surrounded by a playground and a fence, is fast fading into the past.

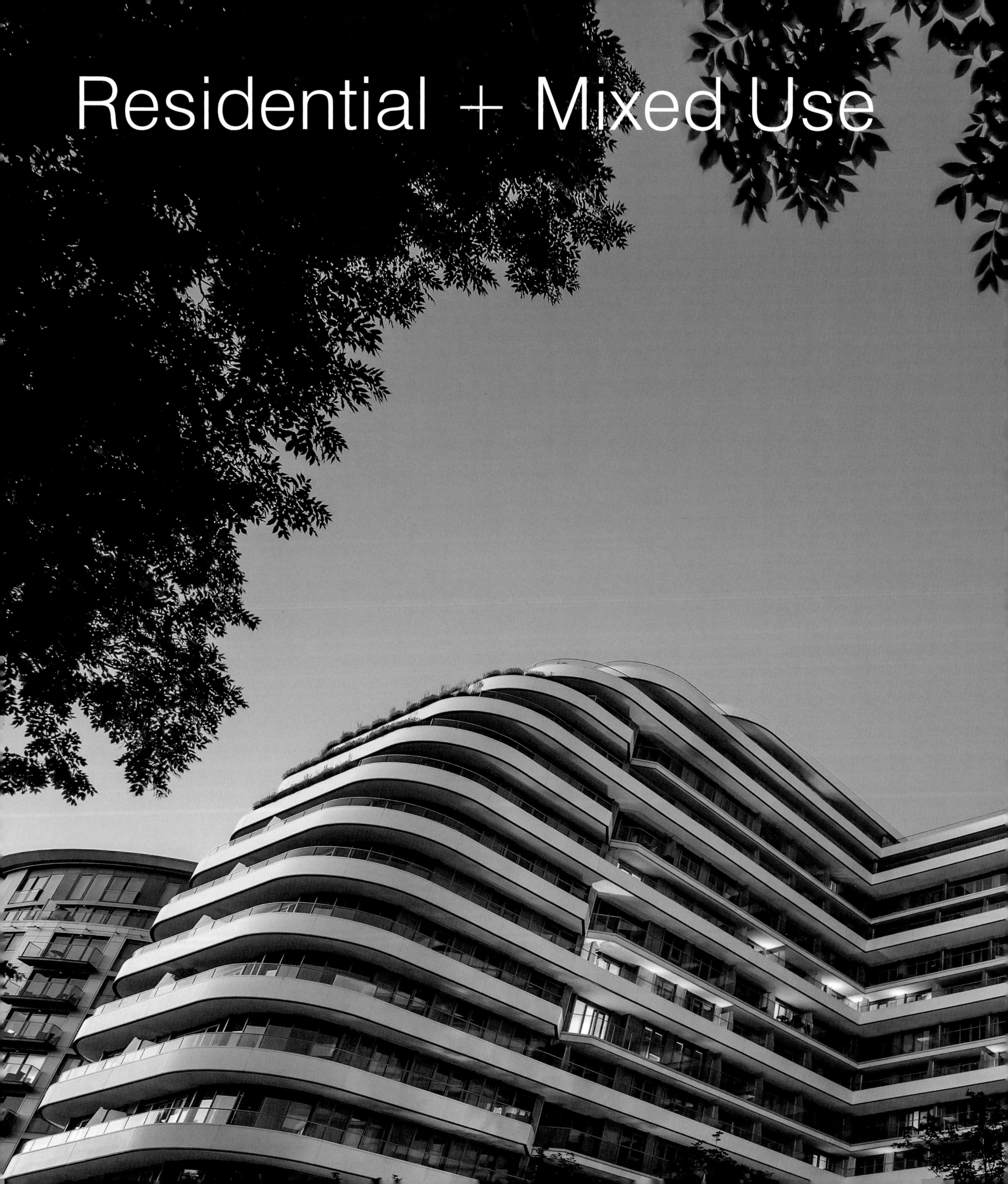

Residential + Mixed Use

Places to live and inhabit

Richard McCarthy

For architects, designing your own house is *the* dream. It is a chance for unconstrained expression of personal style and experimentation. Designing someone else's home is a privilege. You are conspiring and cajoling to practise ideas on the houses of other people – namely, trusting clients. This line of enquiry is so often the starting point for fledgling practitioners, as was the case with John Brownrigg.

Following Annesley Brownrigg's death in 1935, the newly qualified John Brownrigg took over his father's projects and set up his own practice. One of Brownrigg's major interests was in the possibilities of, and various new ways of providing, residential accommodation. He was later instrumental in the research and development of timber-framed prefabricated houses designed for Guildway. Brownrigg was stimulated by natural habitats and materials, exemplified by the house he built for himself and his family in a disused quarry in the centre of Guildford.

A large part of Brownrigg's portfolio at this time consisted of residential projects. He designed numerous housing developments and also private houses, among them a London residence for the racing driver Stirling Moss and a house in Manhattan, New York, for another private client. It is worthwhile exploring here in more detail the Moss residence on account of its sheer ingenuity in so many respects.

In 1961 the Formula 1 British Grand Prix winner Stirling Moss bought a bomb-damaged plot of land nestled in the heart of Mayfair, between Green Park and Park Lane, for £5000. He subsequently appointed Scott Brownrigg & Turner to design a 232-square-metre, five-storey mews house, in which he continued to reside until his later years. Built for £25,000, the modest and understated house is now estimated to be worth at least £10 million.

Moss heavily influenced the house's design, integrating state-of-the-art innovations and technologies that were decades ahead of their time. These included one-way glass fitted in all windows and, on walls throughout, touch-switches that controlled the style and volume of background music, the lighting scheme, intercom system, heating, curtains, floodlights in the garden and even the temperature and depth of the bathwater. An additional feature was a heated toilet seat, which in an interview with the *Sunday Telegraph Magazine* in 1972 he referred to as having 'constant blood heat. Little things like that are what living in the latter part of the 20th century is really about.'

From his office on the ground floor, Moss could talk and listen to anyone in the house, illuminate anyone and, by touching a master button, plunge the whole house into darkness.

In his bedroom Moss incorporated a specially built Myers bed, beside which a control panel allowed him to rule his world while watching a remotely controlled TV set that hung from the ceiling. Mirrored panels in the ceiling above the bed could be folded away to reveal a Nordic solarium for all-over tanning.

A small alcove off the first-floor lounge, referred to as his 'nook', was enclosed by Jacobean-style panelling made of pure fibreglass. At the touch of a switch, sections could be made to slide away, revealing top-of-the-range radio, TV and recording equipment.

At the touch of another switch, a hydraulic wooden dining table, already set for dinner in the kitchen above, could be lowered into the nook, descending through a ceiling panel and returning in the same manner.

The kitchen itself housed a premium cooker and microwave oven, and boiling-hot water was available for use directly out of a tap.

The walls of the infamous lift shaft, which Moss fell down in 2010, were covered with a special spray-on felt fabric to make them look – well, less like the inside walls of a lift shaft.

By 1994 Moss had over 187 different electronic operations within his house. Of his electrical system, he stated in the 1972 interview:

The secret is my low-voltage system. You see when I press this button behind my desk to turn a light on upstairs in the lounge it merely uses a 12-volt circuit. That way I keep the heavy wiring down to a minimum. Even though my wiring looks as complex as the average aircraft, I don't really have any more volts flying about than the normal house. I have been able to indulge in endless combinations of electrical operations without overloading the system.

It is well documented that Moss, a Fellow of the Institute of Engineers, was scrupulously attentive to detail and an advocate of quality. Around 2012–13 he updated and refurbished the Mayfair home.

In 1966, around the same time the Stirling Moss house was designed, the practice was also designing a mixed-use commercial development in the King's Road, Chelsea. Conceived in the International Style, it included a shopping centre built around a pedestrian piazza and surmounted by offices and luxury flats.

As Scott Brownrigg grew to consider more complex projects – building communities rather than building in a community – a conundrum arose: how to translate the craftsmanship and delight of these domestic 'grand designs' to higher densities? This conundrum, grappling with the dynamics of density and place, has been a constant theme of the practice's residential work – one that persists today – and is exemplified by the contrasting scales and densities of the work illustrated in this chapter.

While working on Barrens Park housing scheme in Woking in 1963, partner J. Stanton Abbott observed:

Does the idea of existing in a community have much relevance today? Is one's sense of place reflected in the typical detached unit with its completely introverted enclosure and non-private external area euphemistically called 'garden'? The English Village, the Greek Island Settlement, the Italian Hill Town, all have an inherent unity and direct relationship to the land. The lack of consciousness the public has of its domestic environment has been carefully nursed for years by unimaginative spec building …

On 14 October 1975, Woking's new town centre was officially declared open by the Duchess of Kent in the presence of the client, the president of the Norwich Union Insurance Group. After a brief opening ceremony, the duchess walked around the development for nearly an hour, talking to shoppers, schoolchildren and spectators who had come in their thousands for the occasion. The duchess was accompanied by only two people during her tour, one of whom was Newman Turner.

The completion of this development was a milestone for the practice. It was one of the biggest projects it had certified, and had also been, in many respects, one of the most complex to design and manage up to that point; it was designed during a period of increasing legislation and controls, and constructed during a decade beset with material, labour and energy problems. It consisted of sixty-four shop units, five major department stores, forty-eight apartments and a sixteen-storey air-conditioned office. It instantly became a busy and thriving shopping and commercial centre.

Work on large residential masterplans continued in the mid- to late 1980s with Heron Quays. A project office was established in the heart of London's Docklands to manage the design and construction of future phases of the development, which comprised over 200,000 square metres of commercial, retail and residential space to be delivered over a seven-to-ten-year period. The masterplan for the quay was to provide a '24-hour' environment, with 80,000 square metres dedicated to homes for both the local authority and the private sector.

At a similar time, the practice was involved in the design of ten new Docklands Light Railway stations, using a standard system of components to form a kit of parts, and working with Maunsell as an enabler of and catalyst for this regenerative development. Pertinently, as the practice developed expertise in diverse specialist areas such as transport, commercial property and education, this provided insight into the powerful societal and economic dynamics behind the blending of different uses – living, working, learning and cultural – in the creation of thriving communities.

This productive period for Scott Brownrigg in London Docklands included the preparation on behalf of London and Edinburgh Trust and Tarmac of a masterplan for the development of Royal Albert Dock, at the time one of the largest urban regeneration sites in Europe.

As in the case of many practices in the 1970s, Scott Brownrigg & Turner had started working in the Middle East. It was commissioned by the Qatar Steel Company to design dormitory and senior staff housing to support a new harbour and steel plant in Umm Sa'id Industrial City. The site was 10 kilometres inland on the desert fringes. The community complex was designed to modify the existing harsh external conditions for 650 residents and integrate with the overall industrial development masterplan.

During the 1980s the practice steered away from residential work and focused on commercial offices, international projects and airports. Housing developers of scale in this period rarely employed architects, and architects rarely sullied their good name by being associated with housebuilders. Some of the more interesting housing projects in central London were conceived in-house by the Greater London Council.

However, at the dawn of the twenty-first century this all changed with a large commission on the river in London for Tony Pidgley CBE and his company, Berkeley Group, at Chelsea Bridge Wharf. This was the early days of Berkeley Homes in central London and the start of its mission to buy up old industrial sites along the River Thames and develop longer-term regeneration plans for them.

Chelsea Bridge Wharf was the first building completed as part of the Battersea Power Station and Nine Elms development area, and it helped to position Scott Brownrigg as a leader in developing large-scale, residential-led urban mixed-use projects. Credit is due to Berkeley Group and the London Borough of Wandsworth, which put a great deal of emphasis on the placemaking aspects of the masterplan. A new footbridge under Chelsea Bridge was created to connect Battersea Park to what would become the Battersea Power Station riverside development.

Meanwhile, Marcus Cooper Group bought Ian Pollard's postmodernist Marco Polo House in Queenstown Road in 2006. Having already been commissioned by the previous owner to controversially redevelop the site for residential use, Scott Brownrigg was appointed. Returning to that idea of 'grand designs' and their relationship with higher-density living, the design for Vista (pp. 206–209), as it became known, was inspired by Frank Lloyd Wright's Fallingwater. Like Stirling Moss, Marcus Cooper proved to be an inspiring client, giving the practice free rein to experiment with a design that responded strongly to nature and its park setting. The project received unanimous planning approval, being described by the chair of Wandsworth planning committee as 'a shot in the arm for Nine Elms and Battersea'. Then the site was sold again to Pidgley and his Berkeley Group. The practice was retained to deliver the project, and Berkeley embraced the design concept wholeheartedly. After three clients, the project finally completed in 2018. It was a milestone in the practice's thinking and continues to frame its philosophy for future residential design.

With Vista, Scott Brownrigg strove to break free from the prevailing London vernacular in residential architecture of well-mannered brick boxes with bolt-on balconies, opting instead for taut white bands in a curvilinear, organic form: a building of penthouses with generous gardens in the sky, embracing Battersea Park with clever infinity-style planting – extending the vista, blending views out with the treetops of the park. The shared sunken gardens allow passers-by to enjoy treetop views but shield residents from the noise of the road, and again blur the horizon with the tree-lined park.

A large proportion of Scott Brownrigg's residential work this century has been London regeneration projects, specifically new build on brownfield industrial sites. Owing to the persistent housing shortfall in London and its position as a global city, the costs involved often give residential developers the edge in purchasing prime sites – not just for new build, but also for protected buildings, despite the additional costs of dealing with listed properties or of working in conservation areas.

A commission in 2006 resulted in the conversion of the former campus of Whitelands

Chelsea Bridge Wharf
Chelsea Bridge Wharf was the practice's first project for Berkeley Group, a relationship that has spanned more than twenty-five years.

Cardiff Pointe
The townhouses at Cardiff Pointe are simple yet sophisticated in conception, arranged within a masterplan comprising street, square and landmark.

Whitelands Park
The regeneration of Whitelands College campus includes the refurbishment of a Sir Giles Gilbert Scott building into 100 luxury apartments, and transforms the college chapel into a single luxury home.

College in Putney into an estate of 437 homes. In 2018, working on a conversion with Mount Anvil, the practice turned Hampstead Manor from its use as student accommodation for King's College London into 156 homes. Both projects – known as Whitelands Park and Kidderpore Avenue, respectively – took the measured approach of setting contemporary apartment buildings and townhouses carefully into the grounds, in juxtaposition with the existing Grade II-listed buildings, which were transformed into a collection of bespoke apartments retaining many of the original features and decoration.

By default, many of the regeneration projects Scott Brownrigg has been involved with are waterfront sites owing to their industrial heritage. The practice has become adept at opening up paths and spaces on the water to the public, while ensuring that as many residences as possible can enjoy the views and access. In

this vein, the Cardiff studio led an expansive waterfront masterplan for 640 homes and an International Sports Village on Cardiff Bay, including proposals for two residential towers. The masterplan uses the concepts of street, square and landmark for clear urban legibility. The first phases of modern townhouses, Cardiff Pointe – incorporating distinctive oversized, stack-bonded brickwork – completed in 2016.

The spaces people live in reflect societal habits and rituals at any given place and time. These habits and their aesthetics are heavily influenced by form of production and climate. In fact, society's method of production for housing has changed surprisingly little since the Second Industrial Revolution. The practice has mostly responded to changes in contemporary living by applying technology upgrades to existing typologies; by adding layers of complexity, instead of rethinking the platform.

The Woods (completed 2015) was conceived through the exploration of non-traditional methods of construction, using structurally insulated panels and timber in the design of four contemporary detached houses that echo the same principles that motivated John Brownrigg to work with Guildway in the 1970s. On a remote site in ancient woodland that forms part of a 240-hectare national nature reserve near Woburn, Bedfordshire, they are designed to Passivhaus standard and experiment with spatial arrangements that frame views of the landscape.

Back in Mayfair, modern methods of construction were used to solve the challenges of a significantly constrained urban site. At 3 Down Street Mews (pp. 214–15), the practice built two new townhouses almost entirely out of glass and steel. The residences are a sophisticated study in light and privacy, inspired by the Maison de Verre (1928–32) in Paris, an early experiment in modern living and industrial design. This project – a stone's throw from Stirling Moss's house and similarly packed with innovative gadgets – was a labour of love, running between 2006 and 2020. On completion, the 740-square-metre properties were reported to be the most valuable 'new-build' houses in Mayfair.

In a similar exploration of modern family living, the Singapore studio completed The Strata House in 2020. Designed to sit on a constrained, narrow plot, the house is tailored to its tropical context. Inspired by a play on horizontal strata, it splits and peels in two from a common datum plane, defining upper-storey semi-private spaces while visually connecting lower-storey living areas. The layering of varying heights creates an internal space that weaves around the central steel staircase and connects the family in a fun way.

After opening a studio in New York in 2017, the practice began working on a host of city masterplan ideas. For example, the Financial District Coastal Improvement Program concept

The Woods
The Woods is a series of sustainable homes designed to facilitate a significant reduction in energy consumption and associated costs for residents.

was presented at the World Architecture Festival in Amsterdam in 2018. The scheme is a multifaceted waterfront-improvement initiative that mitigates flood risk, reduces the pollution of New York City's waterways, creates a vibrant, open waterfront, and spurs increased real estate value from Battery Park to Corlears Hook.

When working internationally, Scott Brownrigg takes care to understand the habits, rituals and local forms of production of a place. Housing design and procurement is typically well catered for by local markets, being such an important constituent element of most cities or societal systems. Therefore, clients tend to commission an international architect only when they need to think differently or require different skills to create or tap into a new market. It is within this context that the practice was commissioned to masterplan a new residential hillside settlement in Limassol, Cyprus, anchored to a landmark international school called The Island (pp. 216–19).

While other areas of expertise in the practice, such as aviation, naturally attract a bigger percentage of international projects, over the past decade there has been a surge in masterplanning and concept design for residential and mixed-use projects, particularly in the Middle East, Eastern Europe, and Central and Southeast Asia. Recent work in Azerbaijan is a good example. In 2023, in Baku, Scott Brownrigg began masterplanning 18 square kilometres of land on the Caspian coastline for Emin Agalarov, a forward-thinking entrepreneur with the desire to position Azerbaijan as a sustainable, global destination of the future. The masterplan proposal extends and builds on the success of the existing Sea Breeze development to create a world-class residential, cultural and commercial destination (pp. 220–21). This is a trend that is likely to continue as the practice integrates different areas of expertise with high-density residential experience in order to develop complex urban solutions in new regions and cities.

The Strata House
At The Strata House in Singapore, horizontal aluminium louvres rotated at angles absorb heat from the sun, facilitate air movement within rooms and provide a sense of privacy.

The Strata House
A hammock integrated between floors is an example of a pragmatic yet fun solution to providing daylight and air circulation in a lower-level hallway.

Vista

Wandsworth, London
Completed 2018

Situated on the eastern edge of the Grade II*-listed Battersea Park and adjacent to Chelsea Bridge Wharf, Vista provides over 400 homes and 1300 square metres of commercial space across two contemporary buildings of six to sixteen storeys in height.

Completed in 2018, Vista challenges the traditional idea of amenity space associated with living in central London apartments. The core concept is a building of penthouses, each with a generous garden terrace akin to those found in the leafy suburbs and an infinity-style planted edge treatment that creates a strong connection with the park. The innovative design ensures that, with increased height, the buildings step back to create an organic and curvilinear built form, sensitive in scale and massing to the surrounding conservation area.

The architectural masterplan and landscape design visually extend the park into the development through the use of mature tree planting and the creation of attractive public spaces and visually stimulating recreational space. Vista is a key stepping stone linking the main Nine Elms development area with Battersea Park via a pedestrian route through the site.

Culture has a key part to play in creating successful new places, and Vista incorporates a public art programme that builds on the rich cultural heritage of this important area of London. It ensures that the development has an intrinsic sense of place and identity, while also providing valuable spaces that enhance the experience for all those who live and work in the vicinity.

Artworks include sculptural gardens by Matthew Darbyshire and Nicky Hirst, Pink Floyd lyrics and lines from poems that include local references incorporated into hardscaping, and bark-inspired manifestations by Hirst embedded into the facade of the buildings. Each playfully offers an artistic interpretation of the surrounding landscape or a glimpse into the area's history. The wayfinding across the development, while being smart and informative, incorporates short explanations of the art installations and how they relate to the site, providing context for residents and visitors alike.

The buildings' footprint and their arrangement on-site protect the communal space from the railway. Private terraces feel like an extension of the park, thanks to infinity-style edge planting. Opposite: Location plan with Vista highlighted orange.

Pages 208–209: The unique design ensures that, with increased height, the buildings step back to create a curvilinear built form, sensitive to the setting in scale and massing.

VISTA
Berkeley
020 3053 6900
CIRCUS WEST VILLAGE
BATTERSEA POWER STATION
F45
COMING SOON
F45
COMING SOON
VISTA

Cambium

Wandsworth, London
Completed 2019

The vision for Cambium was to create an inclusive community that incorporates the best principles of quality residential design; to deliver a place where people will aspire to live. Located in Wandsworth, this exemplary urban development makes use of its T-shaped site, while creating a vibrant new community around an urban meadow and a 200-year-old oak tree, believed to have been planted by Capability Brown.

Cambium provides 110 homes, composed of a six-storey apartment block of fifty-five units and a further fifty-five house units across a generous mix of typologies, from starter apartments to innovative courtyard houses and more traditional family townhouses, to accommodate people at different stages of life.

The built form and landscape are driven by a pedestrian and 'domestic-scale' approach, achieved by a sequence of courtyard spaces linked by shared-surface streets connecting to an urban meadow at the heart of the scheme. The development provides plenty of opportunities for residents to come together to enjoy the great outdoors and live life to the full as part of a long-lasting community.

Cambium is one of two residential developments that enabled the rebuild and delivery of the new St John Bosco College in the absence of the originally envisaged Building Schools for the Future funding.

The pedestrian-orientated concept comprises a sequence of courtyard spaces linked by shared-surface mews-type streets to create a quiet, domestic-scale development.

Cambium
The development balances density and usable private space. A historic oak tree, believed to have been planted by Capability Brown, forms the central feature in a new open space.

Down Street Mews

Westminster, London
Completed 2020

The translucent facade of Down Street Mews is inspired by traditional Japanese architectural elements: the light and warmth of *shoji* screens and the privacy of *fusuma* screens. Opposite: Aerial-view drawing.

Down Street Mews explores the parameters of privacy, form and light to create two high-end contemporary residential units on a constricted site in the heart of the Mayfair Conservation Area.

The residences are located in a quiet mews close to Green Park, and have been created through the redevelopment of the former annexe building to the Cavalry and Guards Club.

Enclosed on three sides, the design centres around two courtyards created to allow each dwelling to have three elevations exposed to the east, south and west, thus capturing the most natural daylight possible. The facades are an interpretation of Japanese sliding screens, where white translucent paper provides light, warmth and intimacy, and opaque paper offers privacy.

Like the iconic Maison de Verre in Paris, the two houses use skeleton-frame steel construction to create a free plan and therefore a flexible interior layout that can be divided by permanent or movable screens in each of the upper floors. Generous floor-to-ceiling heights provide further potential to adapt the building for other uses in the future.

Accommodation is spread across four storeys, and there are three additional basement levels that feature a private spa with swimming pool, a sauna, steam rooms, a cinema, a relaxation area, games and utility rooms, passenger lifts and a four-car garage. Outside space includes a 21-square-metre garden patio at ground level and a 116-square-metre roof garden.

Considered by Westminster City Council to be 'an architectural gem' and 'a contemporary addition to the Mayfair Conservation Area', the design set a quality standard that the council planned to cultivate in the borough.

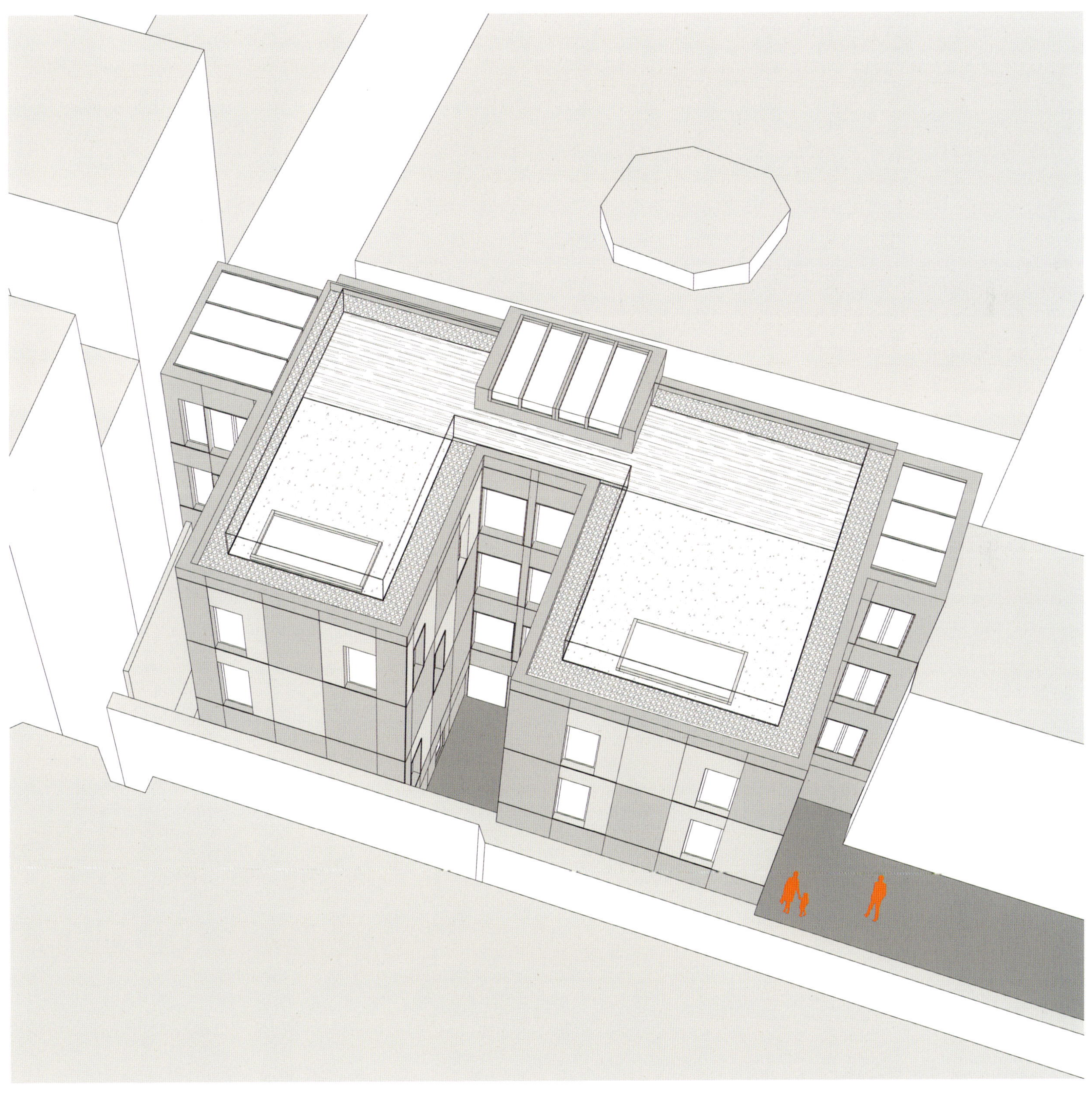

The Island

Limassol, Cyprus
Concept designed
2023

The Island is a 120,000-square-metre mixed-use masterplan comprising 665 high-quality homes interspersed around spaces in which to learn and socialize, setting the scene for a thriving and integrated new community in the semi-mountainous region of Limassol, Cyprus.

The masterplan follows the natural contours of the hillsides, with ecological parklands created on the steepest parts of the slopes and an education hub, residential neighbourhoods and urban centre below.

A central piazza lined with community spaces, a local market, retail and dining spaces will provide both a focal point for the new village and a place for the local and wider community to come together. A range of accessible, versatile and explorable outdoor spaces, combined with a network of foot- and cycle paths, will encourage safe and active travel around the village.

Landscaping strategies seek to restore degraded land through reforestation, erosion control, wetland restoration and terrace farming; to enhance biodiversity through the introduction of native flora and wildlife corridors; and to harvest rainwater via contour swales and mist gardens, creating unique sensory and cooling spaces for the community to explore.

The steeply sloping hillsides of the site, with impressive views towards the surrounding mountains and valleys, have informed the overarching masterplanning principles. Opposite: Masterplan of The Island.

The Island
Landscaping and natural terrain are used to define public and private zones, flowing down steeper parts of the hillside and between buildings to establish strong connections to nature.

Sea Breeze

Baku, Azerbaijan
Concept designed
2023

Positioning Azerbaijan as a sustainable, world-class destination of the future, Sea Breeze promotes a better way of living, working and socializing along the picturesque coast of the Caspian Sea.

Located on 18 square kilometres of land north of Baku, the masterplan builds on the established success of the existing Sea Breeze development to create a highly diverse, inclusive and healthy environment with economic potential to act as an international gateway for commerce and cultural exchange.

As part of the vision, the destination has the potential to produce its own food and energy through such embedded features as solar-energy carpets and vertical-farm hydroponic towers, which combine to assist with self-sufficiency for power and food production. The seamless integration of solar panels and wind-harvesting technology into everyday surroundings will reshape the way we think about energy generation.

The integration of smart-city technologies will amplify the region's significance and transform the Sea Breeze development into an innovative and efficient urban landscape, deeply connected to its cultural and environmental roots; a place where future technologies converge with sustainable practices to create a dynamic and resilient economic model for the future.

Hotels, residential units and a marina combine to create a vibrant centrepiece on a unique crescent-shaped island at the heart of the masterplan.

Future Thinking: Residential + Mixed Use

The future will involve experimenting with increasingly higher-density housing solutions, mitigating the effects of climate change and exploring the plethora of subsectors and residential-tenure models emerging in the West and developing regions. In the UK, safety and increasing regulation following the introduction of the Building Safety Act (after the Grenfell Tower tragedy in 2017) mean there may be less competition as architects struggle to obtain professional indemnity insurance and shy away from the responsibility of delivering their projects. Scott Brownrigg has a long history of designing and delivering projects from concept to completion, and believes that this shift will bring back to the architect responsibility lost during the move towards design-and-build contracts in the 1980s. In much of Europe and in Singapore and the United States, the architect is still responsible for certifying design and carries ultimate responsibility for safety.

Will there be a significant change in the way housing is produced globally? It is hard to say, because society seems wedded to its historical typologies. Will the AI revolution drive societal changes that manifest themselves in the spatial organization of how people live? The start of this change emerged during and following the Covid-19 pandemic, when homes became offices, and having outside space and a quiet place to work became more important.

Grand designs and inspiring architecture will not solve the housing crisis, but – as in the case of high fashion on the catwalk – they can drive innovation and creativity that will eventually find their way into everyday living.

Architects perhaps stand alone in this grandiose view of what a house can represent. The public, and by extension politicians, often have a very different relationship with housing. In conflict zones, access to safe and secure shelter is a fundamental human need, vital for survival. For many in the West, housing is an investment first and a home second; thus, the housing market is intrinsically tied to how people feel about the economy. For most people, home is a refuge, a safe place that is shared with family and friends, one ideally embedded in a community that people can relate to and want to be a part of.

And this is why things change slowly in housing. Notably, only 2 per cent of private homes are commissioned from and designed by architects, so opportunities to innovate must be used wisely.

In other industries, urbanization, technology, climate change, ageing populations and the 'Intelligence Revolution' of AI are driving change and modernization apace. The property industry is slow to react to such trends, and housing appears unperturbed. Disruptors exist; the co-living sector and the build-to-rent market are developing brands to attract millennial tribes and gaining traction with institutional backers. However, it is never going to be easy to break society's obsession with the property ladder.

Housing shortages grab headlines, and politicians and global leaders latch on to the very real challenge of affordability. In the flurry to churn out housing, architects have a duty to stay calm and focus on quality. As human priorities evolve, the spaces people inhabit must adapt to meet new demands. A significant shift is emerging across the key areas discussed below.

There is an increasing emphasis on community-centric design and the provision of communal spaces where multiple families or individuals collaborate to share resources such as energy, transportation, food and water. This approach fosters resilient neighbourhoods capable of operating autonomously during crises, while also enhancing flexibility and the ability to adapt to changing climatic and societal needs.

As urban areas become more crowded and space becomes increasingly scarce, compact, modular and adaptable design is also set to redefine how living spaces are used. These solutions aim to minimize footprints and maximize usability for daily living. Modular construction techniques, when effectively implemented, can streamline building processes, reduce costs and minimize environmental impact by reducing waste and resource consumption.

As advancements in AI and automation continue, smart home systems will play a pivotal role in optimizing how people live. Future homes will integrate intelligent systems that provide seamless control over automation, connectivity and energy efficiency, enhancing every aspect of daily life.

The future of residential design is centred on creating highly efficient, adaptable and sustainable solutions; innovations that prioritize resilience, connectivity and environmental responsibility, all while leveraging the power of cutting-edge technology to improve quality of life. Through design and collaboration, architects have the skills and vision to bring people together and create vibrant places that delight.

Future Thinking

Looking to the future

Darren Comber and Richard McCarthy

In 2025 Scott Brownrigg celebrated 115 years of history. The early twentieth century was a very different time, and from modest beginnings grew a sustainable practice that is today a thriving and influential business with a meaningful place of authority on the international stage. Through its evolution and commitment to continually looking forward, Scott Brownrigg has defined a space within the world of architecture that provides a framework for delivery while respecting the principles on which the practice was founded more than a century ago.

On the wider topic of what may lie ahead, consideration must be given to how architects can avoid sleepwalking into extinction. The AI revolution is in full swing, and – if the hype is to be believed – it may soon be possible to generate the design of a building completely autonomously.

However, the practice has been here before. The long history of Scott Brownrigg suggests that these seismic shifts are never as earth-shattering as first predicted – but they do force evolution and adaptation. Change is constant, but history repeats itself, and human behaviour is cyclical.

AI is driving the Fourth Industrial Revolution, the 'Intelligence Revolution'. The First and Second Industrial Revolutions had a profound effect on architecture. The Second Industrial Revolution introduced new materials and means of production that changed the way the practice constructed and conceived buildings.

Modernism and the International Style compelled Scott Brownrigg to move away from

Financial District Coastal Improvement Program
The Financial District Coastal Improvement Program is a multifaceted waterfront-improvement initiative for New York City facilitated by creating a dual-purpose tunnel that reduces pollution and supports flood mitigation.

New York Wind Turbine
The concept to reinvent Park Avenue's medians with a wind turbine was a finalist in the Experimental Award category at the World Architecture Festival in 2018.

its unassuming beginnings in the Arts and Crafts Movement – a shift that dramatically changed the scale and complexity of the work it undertook. In a book on the history of Scott Brownrigg & Turner published in 1968, there was acknowledgement of the changing role of the architect and a prediction of the rise of the project manager, whose job it would be to deal with coordinating increasingly complex procurement and construction. The architect's evolving role over the decades is another change that Scott Brownrigg has positively embraced, for it brings the opportunity to deliver ever more complex and meaningful projects across the globe as part of a unified team.

The Third Industrial Revolution marked the end of drawing boards, legions of draughtsmen and reams of paper. The digital era fundamentally changed the way designs were produced and communicated. This 'Information Revolution', driven by the digital computer and the internet, continues to transform the way information is accessed and stored; it has led to producing more with less, and faster, and working efficiently across continents, often without even leaving the studio.

Scott Brownrigg has always been at the forefront of the digital era. As one of the first practices to invest in CAD technology in the late 1970s, the company not only embraced the opportunity presented, but sought ways to lead in the field.

The next revolution is an 'Intelligence Revolution'. Architects are seeing the potential of AI, utilizing 'diffusion models' to generate remarkable imagery instantaneously. However, this is the tip of the iceberg. Cognitive technology will potentially be able to powerfully augment and perhaps even surpass human capabilities at all stages of design. Architects will again need to evolve.

It is possible that a shift akin to the demise of the drawing board lies ahead. It could lead to doing even more with even less, but this time perhaps with fewer architects. It is not inconceivable that – with AI doing all the heavy cognitive lifting – a handful of architects with the right skills could compete with the largest firms in the world. But the design process still needs to be curated and creativity judged, and relationships and inputs will still need to be managed. The opportunity ahead is to focus resources where the human consciousness provides the most value.

The architectural profession has given so much away over the past 115 years. AI offers the chance to redesign the profession, and perhaps the opportunity exists to reinvent and reclaim the role of master-builder. In Vitruvian terms, machines cannot for now delight in the experience of the spaces they create, cannot test the firmness of their designs, nor benefit from the commodity of a building and its function.

That said, AI has the power to improve the human connection with products and buildings. Architects will find themselves engaging more with the operational stage of a building's life cycle. How data is processed and collected with intelligent digital twins will also inform how a building adapts over time and how new buildings are designed in response to requirements. This acknowledgement led Scott Brownrigg to develop its own digital twin company, Digital Twin Unit.

Advancements in digital technologies and AI are set to change the way entire industries function. Film studios as a typology, for example, are being transformed as new technologies such as virtual production (VP) and social media algorithms redefine where and how content is created and consumed. Innovative construction techniques enabled Shinfield Studios in Reading to produce a major motion picture while part of the site was still being built. VP is streamlining the spatial requirement of film studios, and the rise of independent film is creating the opportunity to rethink the typology altogether – with the potential to repurpose smaller inner-city spaces and sites as places to support emerging talent.

But architects cannot be successful without clients who are willing to place their trust in them. Traditionally, architects' clients were predominantly the church, royalty, the aristocracy, representatives of empires and political regimes keen to stamp their authority on the world with expressions of power and influence.

In the post-war era, when Scott Brownrigg began to grow, its clients were invariably governments, financial institutions and corporations with similar motivations to provide responses to global trends and emerging industries. Today, however, the practice's clients are diverse; they have multiple drivers, visions and desires, and are not necessarily driven solely by economic circumstances. Over the past thirty years, Scott Brownrigg has seen the traditional big sectors – such as commercial, residential, hospitality and infrastructure – break down into myriad specialist subsectors, each with its own client body and a unique set of dynamics and drivers that require a tailored and respectful response. This pattern of subsectors is developing rapidly, and over the decades Scott Brownrigg has demonstrated the key ability to gain early access to sectors and to nurture the skills that will eventually sustain its future.

The world is facing significant challenges. Globalization is becoming controversial in its contemporary form and must continue to adapt to survive. Architects have a unique brand of skills that bring humanitarian and scientific thought together, leveraging the built environment to support a more equitable future and to exert influence on many world problems, including climate change, health and resource depletion.

The places and spaces of the future must be designed to address these challenges pre-emptively, with a focus on retrofit, renewable energy, biodiversity and the circular economy.

The requirement will be for schemes similar to Scott Brownrigg's vision for the Financial District Coastal Improvement Program, which extends parks in New York City to protect southern Manhattan against future hurricanes, rising tides and flooding; or the New York Wind Turbine concept, which transforms the car-dominated Park Avenue to create moments of delight within the public realm while capturing and storing renewable energy for reuse or deployment elsewhere in the city; or the practice's innovative concept for dynamic cylindrical hydroponic towers that turn and track the sun, generating and capturing renewable energy to power internal vertical farms as they move.

AI presents the opportunity to streamline the spatial requirement of most sectors, but will inevitably increase the demand on data storage. Set to support a new urban code of living and working, data centres will need to be designed to be better neighbours, to ensure a more integrated approach and positive contribution to the natural and built environment.

Across its long history, Scott Brownrigg has demonstrated how architects can adapt to serve societal needs. More generally, architects have a talent for shining a light on how the future might look and feel. Armed with the astonishing power of AI, they have work to do to find solutions to many of the world's problems through the built environment, but the shape of the profession will undoubtedly change as the 'Intelligence Revolution' takes hold. Architects, as 'future gazers', surely can find a way to coexist with humankind's most intelligent creation.

One certainty in the decades ahead for Scott Brownrigg is that the world in which it operates will be a constantly evolving, different place from today. But out of all forms of change, positive opportunities always emerge, whether they be on an environmental, social or economic level. The practice will continue to expand in breadth and depth of knowledge, both responding to and pre-empting societal changes and their impact. While it is not possible to know the extent of the changes and challenges ahead, we do know the importance of acknowledging, embracing and effecting positive change. This recognition is a quality that has guided Scott Brownrigg throughout its decades of progress, and it is one that the practice will continue to use to guide its future.

Contributors

Darren Comber, RIBA, AIA, FRSA, joined Scott Brownrigg in 1995. In 2000 he became the youngest Director in the practice's history to be appointed to the Board of Directors, and he has been the practice's Chief Executive since 2010. He is at the forefront of many of its major UK and international projects.

Richard McCarthy, RIBA, AIA, is a Board Director at Scott Brownrigg. He joined the practice in 1996 and was appointed to the Board of Directors in 2011. He leads the strategic direction of the practice's expertise and portfolio, helping to strengthen the company's position in UK and overseas markets.

Maurice Rosario, RIBA, is the Head of Aviation and a Director at Scott Brownrigg. With an approach grounded in meaningful research, he is an expert in designing and delivering complex global aviation projects, including the world's largest terminal in Istanbul.

Chris Blow, RIBA, FRSA, is a former Partner and Director at Scott Brownrigg, where he specialized in transportation terminals. He is the author of *Airport Terminals* (Butterworth Architecture Library of Planning and Design, 1991; 2nd edn, 1996) and *Transport Terminals and Modal Interchanges: Planning and Design* (2005).

Nick Ridout, RIBA, is the Head of Business Space and a Director at Scott Brownrigg. He leads the design and delivery of a range of high-quality workplaces and major redevelopment schemes across the UK, including in the City of London.

Beatriz Gonzalez is the Head of Workplace Interiors and a Director at Scott Brownrigg. She leads the team in providing evidence-led integrated workplace strategy and interior design solutions for a range of high-profile organizations in the UK and overseas.

Ed Hayden, RIBA, is the Head of Life Sciences and a Director at Scott Brownrigg. He leads the team in providing pioneering, environmentally sustainable environments for life sciences, healthcare and technology companies.

Andrew Postings, RIBA, is the Head of Rail and Infrastructure and a Director at Scott Brownrigg. He is an expert on major infrastructure projects from new-build stations to station modernizations, depots and step-free access, both in the UK and overseas.

Erika Gemmell, RIBA, RIAS, is the Head of Defence and Security and a Director at Scott Brownrigg. She leads the design and masterplanning of all defence- and security-related projects across the practice, both in the UK and overseas.

Ian Pratt, RIBA, is the Head of Education and Healthcare and a Director at Scott Brownrigg. His expertise encompasses projects for learners of all ages and a wide range of educational models, both in the UK and around the world.

Helen Taylor, FRIBA, FRSA, is the Director of Practice at Scott Brownrigg and also specializes in education. She is the co-author of *Urban Schools: Designing for High Density* (2020) and *Community Schools: Designing for Sustainability, Wellbeing and Inclusion* (2023).

Acknowledgements

This book is dedicated to everyone who has worked at Scott Brownrigg over the many decades, contributing to its enduring success; to those who have been instrumental in its growth, and those who continue to help shape the practice for the future. And, of course, to our clients and collaborators, who share our values and vision for creating aspirational architecture that can make a positive impact and stand the test of time.

Special thanks go to our authors – Richard McCarthy, Maurice Rosario, Chris Blow, Nick Ridout, Beatriz Gonzalez, Ed Hayden, Andrew Postings, Erika Gemmell, Ian Pratt and Helen Taylor – and to contributors Alistair Brierley and Nyasa Beale for their insights into key areas of the practice and how each has developed and evolved over time.

We would also like to thank the team at Merrell Publishers – Hugh Merrell, Nicola Bailey and Claire Chandler – and our own marketing team at Scott Brownrigg – Claire Donald, Harriet Methven and Rebecca Williams – for coordinating, editing and producing the book. Thanks also to all the photographers who have so beautifully captured our projects through a lens.

Darren Comber, CEO

Picture Credits

Arup/Daniel Imade: 124
Aspire Defence: 157
David Barbour: cover, 44–45, 56, 57, 144, 148–49, 150–51, 160, 162–63, 188–89 top
David Churchill: 23
Martin Cleveland: 53, 54–55, 104
UK MoD © Crown copyright 2025: 154–55
Philip Durrant: 68–69, 75, 76, 76–77, 84–85, 85, 86–87, 88–89, 89, 140–41, 152–53
Gifford: 118–19, 128–29, 130–31
Richard Gooding Photography: 132–33
Ashley Goodwin: 146, 202 left
Google Earth, 2025 Airbus: 30
Nick Guttridge: 73
Adrian Hobbs: 173
Andrew Holt/Alamy Stock Photo: 48
Hundven-Clements Photography: 47, 58, 58–59, 61, 62–63, 64 top, 65, 92–93, 98, 100–101, 107, 108–109, 167 left and right, 169, 174–75, 175, 181, 182–83, 184–85, 186, 186–87, 190, 191 top, 192–93, 196–97, 202 right, 203, 206, 208–209
IGA Istanbul Airport: 34
Mike Jones: 16
Khoo Guo Jie: 204, 205
LEH Foshan: 171
McLaren Construction Group PLC: 210, 210–11, 212–13
Jeffrey Milstein: 28
Monkey Business Images: 180 top
Adrian Pink via Flickr: 28–29
Aaron Pocock: 170, 176–77, 177, 178–79
Liane Ryan Photography: 82, 82–83
Jim Stephenson: 24, 35, 36–37
Edmund Sumner: 95
Alicia Taylor: 74
Transport for London: 134, 134–35
Philip Vile: 80–81, 81
Anthony Weller, Archimage: 50
Alex Winship Photography: 214
Alex Wroe (2019): 71

The artwork shown on pp. 134–35 is Daniel Buren's *Diamonds and Circles*, permanent work *in situ*, Tottenham Court Road station, London, 2017.

Index

Page numbers in *italic* refer to the illustrations.

Abbey Wood, Filton, Bristol 142–44, *143*, 145
Abbott, J. Stanton 199
Aberdeen 170–71, *188–89*, 189
ABP 170
Abu Dhabi 10, 70, 171
Abu Dhabi Trade Centre *46*, 47
Academies Programme 167
Acanthus Architects LW 123
Acorn Computers 99
Adaptable Base Build Concept 66
Adelaide House, London 51, 73
AECOM 123, 126, 128
Africa 10
Agalarov, Emin 204
AI (artificial intelligence) 222, 223, 226, 229–31
Air Russia hub, Moscow Domodedovo Airport 22
Airbus A380 24, 28
airports 18–43
Al Nahyan, Sheikh Suroor bin Mohammed 47
Aldershot, Hampshire 144–45, 156, *160*
Almacantar 70
Amathus Beach Hotel, Limassol, Cyprus 75
Amsterdam 13, 72, 204
Angel Building, London 72, 82
Antalya Airport, Turkey 24
Apple 99
Architectural Association (AA) 7, 8
Arlington Securities 72, 94
Arm Headquarters, Cambridge 51, 60, *60–63*, 72, 74, 99, 114
Arora Group 25
Arts and Crafts Movement 46, 73, 229
Arup 123
Ashchurch, Gloucestershire 147
Ashford, Kent 164, *165*
Aspire Defence 144, 156
Assembly Hotel, Leicester Square, London 75
Associated British Consultants 8
aviation 18–43
Aviva 48
Ayios Nikolaos Station, Cyprus 142
Aylesford School Sports College 164, 166
Azerbaijan 204, 220–21

Baghdad International Airport, Iraq 22
Bahrain Airport 22
Bain & Company 70
Baker McKenzie 70
Baku, Azerbaijan 204, 220, *220–21*
Balls, Ed 166
Bangkok 24, 123
Bank of England 66, 73
Barings Bank 50
Barney, Gerry 120, *121*
Bartley Wood Business Park, Hook 96
Basra Airport, Iraq 22
Battersea Power Station, London 200–201
Bauhaus 13
Bawden, Edward 122
BBC White City, London 12, *48*, 49
BEA (British European Airways) 14
Beckton, London 120
Beijing 98–99
Belgrade 72
Berkeley Group 200–201
25 Berkeley Square, London 73
Birmingham 'Eurohub' 22
Bishopsgate, London 50
Black, Misha 121, 122
Blythe Valley Park, Solihull 97
BMW 96
BOAC Terminal, JFK Airport, New York 14, *15*, 24
Boeing aircraft 14, 21, 24, 28, 70
Bournemouth 75
BP Sunbury 58, *58–59*, 71
Bracknell 94
Bridgend, Wales 167
Bridgwater, Somerset 166
Bristol 167
British Airports Authority (BAA) 20
British Airways 14, 21, 27
British Army 7, 142, 144–47
British Construction Industry Regeneration Award 128
British Council for Offices (BCO) 14–15, 49, 51, 56, 73, 81, 97
British Council for School Environments 166
British Land 97, 99
British Rail 120–21, *121*
British Safety Council 145
500 Brook Drive, Reading 49, 56, *56–57*, 73, 78, 97, 102
Brownrigg, Annesley 7, 46, 198
Brownrigg, John 8, *12*, 164, 198, 203
Browns restaurant, St Martin's Lane, London 74
Brunel, Isambard Kingdom 13, 126
Building Design magazine 48
Building Schools for the Future (BSF) 164, 166, 168, 210
Burberry 11
Bureau d'Études Technip 22–23
Buren, Daniel 126, 134, *134–35*
business and science parks 92–116

CABI Headquarters, Wallingford 15, 51, *64–65*, 65, 73
Cadbury 73
Cairo Airport *23*, 24
Cam Ranh, Vietnam 22
Cambium, Wandsworth, London 210, *210–13*
Cambridge 116
  Arm Headquarters 51, 60, *60–63*, 72, 74, 99, 114
  Cambridge Biomedical Campus 99, *100–101*
  Cambridge International Technology Park 99, 114, *114–15*
  Cambridge Lakes 97
  Cambridge Science Park 97–99, 106, *106–109*
  The Optic 99, 114
  Peterhouse Technology Park 114, *114*
  Three Crowns House 97
Canary Wharf, London 15, 72, *88–89*, 89
Cardiff Pointe 202, *202*
Carillion 123
Caspian Sea 220
Castrol House, Marylebone, London 13
Cathay Pacific 22
Celgene 70, 71
Central Asia 204
Central Saint Martins, London 75
Centrica 70, 71
28 Chancery Lane, London 51
Channel 4 166
Charles, Prince of Wales 21
Chartis Insurance 70
Chaucer Insurance 72
Cheapside House, London 50
Chek Lap Kok, Hong Kong International Airport 22
Chelsea Bridge Wharf, London 200–201, *201*, 206
Chilton Trinity Technology College, Bridgwater 166
Chilworth, Surrey 164
China 22, 123, 171

Cisco 70
City of London 13, 15–17, 50, 60, 66
Cobham, Surrey 164
Coleg Cymunedol Y Dderwen Comprehensive School, Bridgend 167
Comber, Darren 6, 7, 166
Commercial Union Tower, London 13–14, *14*, 50
Commission for Architecture and the Built Environment 166
Computacenter, Hatfield 94–95
computer-aided design (CAD) 11–12, 20, 22, 229
Concorde 14, 21, 27
Condé Nast Traveller magazine 21
Cooper, Marcus 201
Copenhagen Metro *122*, 123
Costain 170
Covent Garden, London 10, 14, 47
Covid-19 pandemic 65, 66, 194, 222
Croatia 70
Croydon 167–68, *167*
Cumberland Hotel, London 75, 85
Curtelin Ricard Bergeret 22–23
Cyprus 10, 75, 142, 171, 194, 204, 216, *216–19*

Daily Telegraph 21, 48
Darbyshire, Matthew 206
Debden, Essex 171
defence 140–61
Defence Estate Optimisation Programme 161
Delhi 22
Dennis Lau & Ng Chun Man 122
Department for Education (DfE) 167, 168, 194
Department of the Environment 52, 142
Design Centre, London 121
Design Delivery Unit 10
Design Management Unit 10
Design Research Unit (DRU) 10, 13, 120–23, *121*
Design Strategy Unit 10, 71, 82
Diana, Princess of Wales 21
Digital Twin Unit 10, 230
Dining Wall Café, London *16*, 17
Diori Hamani International Airport, Niger 24
Ditton Park Academy, Slough 168–69
Docklands, London 15, *17*, 200
Docklands Light Railway (DLR), London 120, 128, *128–31*, 200
Down Street Mews, London 203, 214, *214–15*
DSSR 20
Dubai 72, 82
Dyson 11

East Malling, Kent 164, 166
Eastern Electricity 70
Eastern Europe 204
Eastpoint Business Park, Oxford 99
Eden House, London 50
Edinburgh 168
education 162–95
EduCity Iskandar, Malaysia 177
Egham, Surrey 51, 73, *73*
EgyptAir 24
Eli Lilly 70, 71
Elizabeth, The Queen Mother 164
Elizabeth II, Queen 8, 142, 148
Ellington School for Girls, Ramsgate 164
The Elmgreen School, Lambeth, London 166, 168, 172, *172–73*
Elysium Beach Resort, Paphos, Cyprus 75
Enfield *124*
English Heritage 133, 169
English Property Corporation 47
Environment Agency 14, 49, 52, 96
Erbil Airport, Kurdistan 22
ExCeL London 120, 128
Expedia 71, 72, 82, *82–83*

Fallingwater, Pennsylvania 201
Filton, Bristol 142–44, *143*
financial crisis (2008–2009) 98, 168
Financial District Coastal Improvement Program, New York 203–204, *226–27*, 231
Finlay, James & Co. 47
First World War 7
Fordham, Max 168
Foreign, Commonwealth and Development Office (FCDO), Buckinghamshire 142, 145
Foundation Park, Maidenhead *96*, 97, *98*
France 22–23
Free Trade Hall, Manchester 74–75
Freeman Fox 122
Frimley, Surrey 94
Frogmore Real Estate Partners Investment Managers 97

G-Research, Soho, London 72, 74
Gallagher, Arthur J. 73, *80–81*, 81
Galliford Try 168
Games, Abram 122
Gartner 51, 73, *73*
Gatwick Airport, Pier 6 24, 28, *28–29*
GDS software 12
Gdynia, Poland 72
Germany 13, 82, 144
Gilwell Park, Epping Forest 194
Glasgow 8, 47
Gollins Melvin Ward (GMW) 13–14, 24, 50
Goodman 72, 94
Google 70, 72, 76, *76–77*
Great Zimbabwe 24
Greater London Council 20, 200
Green & Black's 73
Green Park, Reading 49, 56, 97, 102, *102–103*
Green Park House, Mayfair, London 73
Greenwich, London 152, *152–53*, 161
Gropius, Walter 13, 75
The Guardian 49
Guildford, Surrey 8, 13, 14, 46, 198
  Guildford Business Park 94
  Queen Elizabeth Barracks 8, 142
  Surrey Police Headquarters 145
  Yvonne Arnaud Theatre 11, *12*
Guildway 198, 203
GVA 70

Hail Airport, Saudi Arabia 23
Hamburg 72, 82
Hampstead Manor, London 202
Hampton, London 171
Harare, Zimbabwe 10, 24
Hard Rock Hotel London 75, *75*, *84–87*, 85
Harlow, Essex 169
Harris Invictus Academy, Croydon 167–68, *167*
Haslemere, Surrey 7, 46
Haslemere Hall 46
Hatfield, Hertfordshire
  Computacenter 94–95
  Hatfield Aerodrome 94
  Hatfield Business Park 70
  T-Mobile Headquarters 95–96, *95*
Heathrow Airport 20
  Heathrow West 25, *25*, 38, *38–41*, 43
  Terminal 1 20
  Terminal 3 24, 27
  Terminal 4 11, 20–21, *21*, *26–27*, 27
Heron Quays, Docklands, London 15, *17*, 200
Hersham, Surrey 167, *167*, 184, *184–87*
Hillingdon, London 166
Hillview School for Girls, Tonbridge 168
Hilton Terrace Mount, Bournemouth 75
Hirst, Nicky 206
Hiscock, Leslie 7–8, *9*
Hitchin Centre, North Hertfordshire College *169*, 170, *174–75*, 175
Holden, Charles 125
Holiday Inns 75
Holmesdale School, Snodland 164, 166
Hong Kong 122–23, 138
  Chek Lap Kok Airport 22
  Kwun Tong line 122
  Mass Transit Railway (MTR) 122, 123
  Modified Initial System (MIS) 122
  Queen's Hill Camp 142
Hook, Hampshire 96
housing 196–223
The Howard Partnership Trust 184
Howbery Business Park, Wallingford 96, 104, *104–105*
HR Wallingford Group 96, 104
Hub South East Scotland 168
Hugh Christie Technology College, Tonbridge 164
Hull 71–72, *71*, 73
Huntingdon, Cambridgeshire 154, *154–55*
Hyatt House, Stratford, London 75
Hyatt Regency, Stratford, London *74*, 75

Industrial Revolutions 226, 229
'Intelligence Revolution' 222, 226, 229–31

interior design 68–91
International Style 199, 226–29
IPWC 71
IRA 50
Iraq 10, 22
Iraqi State Organization for Roads and Bridges 22
Iskandar Puteri, Malaysia 170, *170*, *176–79*, 177
Islam 31
The Island, Limassol, Cyprus 216, *216–19*
Island Private School, Limassol, Cyprus 171, 194, 204
Istanbul Airport 24, *24*, *34–37*, 35
Istanbul Atatürk Airport 24

James, Sebastian 168
Jersey 75
JFK Airport, New York 14, *15*, 24
Johnson, Boris 96
Johnson Matthey 169
Jordan 72, 82
Jubail, Saudi Arabia 48

Kent, Duchess of 200
Kent Schools 164–65, *165*
Kestrel House, Wallingford 96, 104, *104–105*
Khalifa University, Abu Dhabi 171
Kidderpore Avenue, London 202
King, Mike 20
King Khalid International Airport, Riyadh, Saudi Arabia 23
King's College London 202
King's Road, Chelsea, London 199
King's Troop Royal Horse Artillery, Greenwich, London 152, *152–53*, 161
Kuala Lumpur Sepang Airport 24
Kurdistan 22

Lady Eleanor Holles (LEH) School, Hampton 171
Lambeth Building Schools for the Future 166, 172
Lancaster University Library Extension 170
Land Securities 70
Learning and Skills Council 164, 167
LEH Foshan, China 171, *171*
Letchworth Studio School 170, 175
Liberty Property Trust 97
Limassol, Cyprus 75, 171, 194, 204, 216, *216–19*
Lincolnshire 168
Lloyds Banking Group 72
Local Education Partnerships 168
67 Lombard Street, London 51
London: Adelaide House 51, 73
  Angel Building 72, 82
  Assembly Hotel, Leicester Square 75
  BBC White City 12, *48*, 49
  25 Berkeley Square 73
  Bishopsgate 50
  Browns restaurant, St Martin's Lane 74
  Cambium, Wandsworth 210, *210–13*
  5 Canada Square, Canary Wharf 72, *88–89*, 89
  Castrol House, Marylebone 13
  Central Business District (CBD) 15
  28 Chancery Lane 51
  Cheapside House 50
  Chelsea Bridge Wharf 200–201, *201*, 206
  Commercial Union Tower 13–14, *14*, 50
  Covent Garden 14, 47
  Dining Wall Café *16*, 17
  Docklands 15, *17*, 200
  Docklands Light Railway (DLR) 120, 128, *128–31*
  Down Street Mews 203, 214, *214–15*
  Eden House 50
  The Elmgreen School, Lambeth 166, 168, 172, *172–73*
  G-Research, Soho 74
  Google 72, 76, *76–77*
  Green Park House, Mayfair 73
  Hard Rock Hotel London 75, *75*, *84–87*, 85
  Heron Quays, Docklands 15, *17*, 200
  Hyatt House, Stratford 75
  Hyatt Regency, Stratford *74*, 75
  Kidderpore Avenue 202
  King's Troop Royal Horse Artillery, Greenwich 152, *152–53*, 161
  67 Lombard Street 51
  London City Airport 128, 170
  41 Lothbury 50–51
  Marco Polo House 201
  Meridian Water station, Enfield 123, *124*
  Mulberry UTC 169–70
  10 Old Burlington Street 72
  Paddington Bakerloo line station 123, 126, 136, *136–37*, 138
  Piccadilly line 21, 124, 125, *132–33*, 133
  Puddle Dock 51
  Rennie House, Blackfriars 46–47
  Rokeby Boys' School, Canning Town 166
  Royal Albert Dock 170, 200
  Ruislip High School, Hillingdon 166
  St Paul's Cathedral 13, 49, 51, 66
  Sarah Bonnell School for Girls, Stratford 166
  Scott Brownrigg offices 14
  South Thames College, Wandsworth 167
  Stirling Moss house, Mayfair 198–99
  Tottenham Court Road station 123, 125–26, 134, *134–35*
  Tower 42 50
  University of Westminster 170
  Vista, Wandsworth 201, 206, *206–209*
  Walbrook Building 73, *80–81*, 81
  Warnford Court 73
  Whitelands Park, Putney 201–202, *202*
  see also Gatwick Airport; Heathrow Airport
London Design and Engineering UTC 170
London and Edinburgh Trust 200
London Stock Exchange Group (LSEG) 72
London Transport Executive 120, 121–22
London Underground 21, 121–22, 124–26, *132–37*, 133, 134, 136
Long Thanh Airport, Vietnam 22
Lonrho 50
Los Angeles 9
41 Lothbury, London 50–51
Lothians, Scotland 168
Luton, Bedfordshire *146*, 147, 170
Lyneham, Wiltshire 146–47
Lyon-Saint Exupéry Airport 23
Lyons Corner Houses 85

McCartney, Stella 75
McQueen, Alexander 75
Magdalen College, Oxford 100
Maidenhead, Berkshire *96*, 97, *98*
Maine, John 125, 133
Maison de Verre, Paris 203, 214
Malaysia 170
The Malling School, East Malling 164, 166
Maltings Academy, Witham 167
Manchester 12, 22, 74–75
Manhattan, New York 198
Mapletree 102
Marco Polo House, London 201
Marcus Cooper Group 201
Marham, Norfolk 145
Maunsell 22, 120, 122–23, 200
Medina, Saudi Arabia 23, *30–33*, 31
Merchants' Academy Primary School, Bristol 167
Meridian Water station, Enfield 123, *124*
MicroGDS software 12
Middle East 10, 22, 23, 31, 70, 72, 82, 200, 204
Mies van der Rohe, Ludwig 13
Milltimber Primary School, Aberdeen 171, *188–89*, 189
Milton Keynes, Buckinghamshire *50*, 51, 73
Mini 11
Ministry of Defence (MoD) 142–48, 154, 161
Ministry of Works 8
mixed use and residential 196–223
modernism 7, 12, 13, 50, 125, 133, *226–29*
Morgan, J.P. 97
Morgan Est 125
Morgan Sindall 126
Morreau, C.J. 8
Moscow 22, 70
Moss, Stirling 198–99, 201, 203
Mount Anvil 202
Mowlem, John 142
Mulberry UTC, London 169–70
Muller, Mike 99
Munich 72, 82
Mutual Investment Model 164
Myerson, Jeremy 144

National Education Nature Park 194
National Maritime Systems Centre, Portsmouth 147

National Theatre, London 170
Natural England 194
NBCUniversal 71
NCR 72
Network Rail 51, 126
Network Rail National Centre, Milton Keynes *50*, 51
New City College, Epping Forest, Debden 171
New Rickstones Academy, Witham 167
New York 13, 72, 89, 198
BOAC Terminal, JFK Airport 14, *15*, 24
Financial District Coastal Improvement Program 203–204, *226–27*, 231
New York Wind Turbine *228*, 231
New Zealand 9
Newbury, Berkshire 166
Newcastle University 170
Newham, London 166, 170
Newton, Ernest 7
Niger 24
Nine Elms, London 200–201, 206
Non-Aligned Movement conference, Baghdad (1982) 22
North Africa 23, 31
North Hertfordshire College *169*, 170, *174–75*, 175
The North School, Ashford 164, *165*
Northwood, Middlesex *144*, 145, 148, *148–51*
Norwich Union Insurance Group 200
Nottingham 72, 123
NTL 96

The Office Group 70
offices 44–67
10 Old Burlington Street, London 72
Old Mutual 96
Olympia & York 15
Olympic Games, London (2012) 125, 128, 133
Oman 171
One Canada Square, London 15
The Optic, Cambridge 99, 114
Optimum Schools model 168, 169
Oracle Headquarters, Thames Valley Park 49, *49*, 96
Oriana, SS 120
Otkritie Bank 70
Oxford 99, 116
The Oxford Science Park 99–100, 110, *110–13*
Oxford Brookes University 169

P&O Orient Line 120
Paddington Bakerloo line station, London 123, 126, 136, *136–37*, 138
Pakistan 8, 9
Paolozzi, Sir Eduardo 134
Paris 14–15, 203, 214
Passivhaus 203
Paxton, Joseph 13
PE Consulting Services 48
Pelli, César 15
Permanent Joint Headquarters (PJHQ), Northwood *144*, 145, 148, *148–51*
Peterborough 7, 8, 164
Peterhouse Technology Park, Cambridge 51, 60, 114, *114*
Piccadilly line, London 21, 124, 125, *132–33*, 133
Pidgley, Tony 200, 201
Plymouth, Devon 142
Poland 72
Pollard, Ian 201
Portsdown Technology Park, Portsmouth 147
Portsmouth 142, 147
postmodernism 12, 201
Prince Mohammad bin Abdulaziz International Airport, Saudi Arabia 23, *30–33*, 31
Priority School Building Programme 164, 168
Project Allenby Connaught 144–45, 156, *156–60*
Project Pride, RAF Wyton, Huntingdon 154, *154–55*
Project Winfra 147
Property Services Agency 142
PRUPIM 49, 97, 102
Puddle Dock, London 51
Pugh, Gareth 75

Al-Qassim Airport, Saudi Arabia 23
Qatar Steel Company 200
The Quadrant, Network Rail National Centre, Milton Keynes *50*, 51
Queen Elizabeth Barracks, Guildford 8, 142
Queen's Hill Camp, Hong Kong 142
Quintiles 49, 70, 73, 78, *78–79*

Radisson Blu Waterfront Hotel, St Helier, Jersey 75
Radisson Edwardian Hotel, Manchester 74–75
rail 118–39
Ramsgate, Kent 164
Reading, Berkshire: 500 Brook Drive 49, 56, *56–57*, 73, 78, 97, 102
Green Park 49, 56, 97, 102, *102–103*
Quintiles 78, *78–79*
Theale HQ 72
University of Reading 170
Reckitt Benckiser Science and Innovation Centre, Hull 71–72, *71*, 73
Red Kite House, Wallingford 49, 52, *52–55*, 96–97, 104, *104–105*
Reed's School, Cobham 164
Rees, Peter 50–51
Refinitiv 72
Rennie House, Blackfriars, London 46–47
Renzo Piano Building Workshop (RPBW) 126, 136
residential and mixed use 196–223
Rhodium, Blythe Valley Park, Solihull 97
Riyadh, Saudi Arabia 23, 72
Rokeby Boys' School, Canning Town, London 166
Roshn 72
Royal Air Force (RAF) 8, 142, 147
Royal Albert Dock, London 170, 200
Royal Commission for Jubail and Yanbu 48
Royal London 50, 51
Royal Mail 94, 126
Royal Naval Air Station (RNAS) Yeovilton 147
Royal Navy 8, 142, 147, 148
Ruislip High School, Hillingdon, London 166

Safety Design Unit 10
Sainsbury, J. 47
St Athan, Wales *145*, 146–47
St Bartholomew's School, Newbury 166
St George's College, Weybridge 171, 190, *190–93*
St Helier, Jersey 75
St John Bosco College, London 210
St Paul's Cathedral, London 13, 49, 51, 66
Salisbury Plain 144, 156
Sarah Bonnell School for Girls, Stratford, London 166
Saudi Arabia 23, *30–33*, 31, 48, 72
School Rebuilding Programme 164
schools 162–95
science and business parks 92–116
Scott, Duncan 8, *9*
Scott Brownrigg: architectural styles 12–13
brand perception 11
clients 230
environmentalism 14–15
history 7–17
international projects 9–10, 13
specialist services 10–11
urban design 15
see also individual projects
Scott Brownrigg & Turner (SBT) 8–9, *9*, 10
Scott Wilson Kirkpatrick 22
Scout Association Headquarters, Gilwell Park, Epping Forest 194
Sea Breeze, Baku, Azerbaijan 204, 220, *220–21*
Sealink 121
Second World War 8, 152
Sellar Properties 126, 136
Serbia 72
Shaw, Jonathan 166
Shinfield Studios, Reading 230
'Silicon Fen' 99
Silk Road 22
Sinan, Mimar 35
Singapore 13, 138, 170, 177, 222
Mass Rapid Transit (MRT) system 126–27
The Strata House 203, *204–205*
Sir Charles Kao UTC, Harlow 169
Slough, Berkshire 168–69
Snodland, Kent 164, 166
Solihull 97
South Thames College, Wandsworth 167
Southampton Solent University 170, 180, *180–83*

Southeast Asia 22, 177, 204
Soviet Union 22
The Spark, Southampton Solent University 170, 180, *180–83*
Spitalfields Market Development Area, London 50
Stamford, Connecticut 72, 89
State Street 72
Stevenage Studio School 170, 175, *175*
Stoneywood Primary School, Aberdeen 171, 189
Stora Enso 66
The Strata House, Singapore 203, *204–205*
Stratford, London 75
Sunbury-on-Thames, Surrey 58, *58–59*, 71
Sunday Telegraph Magazine 198
Sunday Times 75
Surrey Police Headquarters, Guildford 145
Swindon UTC 169
SWK 20
Symantec Campus, Reading 97, 102, *103*

T-Mobile Headquarters, Hatfield 70, 95–96, *95*
Taif Airport, Saudi Arabia 23
Tamesis, Egham 51, 73, *73*
Tanzania 164
Tarmac 200
Teach the Future 194
Ted Baker 75
Thames, River 200
Thames Tideway Tunnel 170
Thames Valley 94
Thames Valley Park 49, *49*, 96
Thames Water 170
Thatcher, Margaret 15
Theale HQ, Reading 72
Thomson Reuters 71, 72, *88–89*, 89
Three Crowns House, Cambridge 97
Three Rivers Academy, Hersham 167, *167*, 184, *184–87*
Tidworth Garrison, Wiltshire *157–59*
Tillingbourne School, Chilworth 164
Timber Office Concept 66–67
The Times 21, 48
Times Square, New York 72
Tonbridge, Kent 164, 168
Toshiba UK 94
Tottenham Court Road station, London 123, 125–26, 134, *134–35*
Tower 42, London 50
Transport for London (TfL) 125, 136
Trinity College, Cambridge 97
Tube Lines 124–25
Tungsten, Blythe Valley Park, Solihull 97
Turkey 24, 35
Turner, Gavin 144
Turner, Newman 8, 200
TusPark (Tsinghua University Science Park), Beijing 98–99

Umm Sa'id Industrial City, Qatar 200
United States of America 13, 72, 222
University of Cambridge 97–98
University of East London 120, 170
University of Hertfordshire 94
University of Luton 170
University of Reading 170
University of Reading Malaysia, Iskandar Puteri 170, *170*, *176–79*, 177
University of Sheffield 13
University of Surrey 170
University Technical Colleges (UTCs) 169
University of Westminster, London 170

Venturers' Academy, Bristol 167
Victoria Gate, Woking *47*, 48, 73
Victoria line, London 121–22
Vietnam 22
Vista, Wandsworth, London 201, 206, *206–209*
VLSI Technology 99
Volkswagen 72
VW Financial Services, Milton Keynes 73

Walbrook Building, London 73, *80–81*, 81
Wales 167
Wallingford, Oxfordshire: CABI Headquarters 15, 51, *64–65*, 65, 73
  Environment Agency 14
  Howbery Business Park 96, 104, *104–105*
  Kestrel House 96, 104, *104–105*
  Red Kite House 49, 52, *52–55*, 96–97, 104, *104–105*
Warnford Court, City of London 73
Watchmoor Park, Frimley 94
Waterside Park, Bracknell 94
Wells Cathedral 190
West Nile Street, Glasgow 47
Westminster Bank, Haslemere 46
Westminster City Council 214
Westminster County Court 74
Weybridge, Surrey 171, 190, *190–93*
White City, London 12, *48*, 49
Whitelands Park, Putney 201–202, *202*
Winterbourne Academy, Gloucestershire 167
Witham, Essex 167
Woburn, Bedfordshire 202–203, *203*
Woking, Surrey 8, *47*, 48, 73, 199–200
The Woods, Woburn 202–203, *203*
'Workplace 2000' 48–49
Workstyle Profiler 71
Worktech conference (2017) 71
World Architecture Festival 35, 171, 204, 228
Wright, Frank Lloyd 201
WSP 126
Wyton, Cambridgeshire 145, 154, *154–55*

Yvonne Arnaud Theatre, Guildford 11, *12*

Zimbabwe 10, 24

First published 2025 by Merrell Publishers,
London and New York

Merrell Publishers Limited
70 Cowcross Street
London EC1M 6EJ
merrellpublishers.com

British Library Cataloguing in Publication Data.
A catalogue record for this book is available from the British Library.

ISBN 978-1-8589-4722-8

Produced by Merrell Publishers Limited
Designed by Nicola Bailey
Project-managed by Claire Chandler
Proofread by Barbara Roby
Indexed by Hilary Bird

Printed and bound in China

Cover: 500 Brook Drive, Green Park, Reading, Berkshire; see pp. 56–57.

Pages 18–19: Heathrow West, Heathrow Airport, Hillingdon, London; see pp. 38–41.

Pages 44–45: 500 Brook Drive, Green Park, Reading, Berkshire; see pp. 56–57.

Pages 68–69: Volkswagen Financial Services, Milton Keynes, Buckinghamshire, completed 2015.

Pages 92–93: Plots 1–21, Cambridge Science Park, Cambridge; see pp. 106–109.

Pages 118–19: Langdon Park station, Docklands Light Railway, London; see pp. 128–31.

Pages 140–41: King's Troop Royal Horse Artillery, Greenwich, London; see pp. 152–53.

Pages 162–63: Milltimber School, Aberdeen; see pp. 188–89.

Pages 196–97: Vista, Wandsworth, London; see pp. 206–209.

Pages 224–25: Sea Breeze, Baku, Azerbaijan; see pp. 220–21.